START HERE

Why JESUS Came
and How His Message Gives You LIFE

D0907461

By Jeff Struecker

All Bible references are from the *Christian Standard Bible* (*CSB*) unless otherwise specified.

Edited by Readable Reach: www.readablereachbooks.com

Start HERE: Why Jesus Came and How His Message Gives You Life/ Jeff Struecker. -- 1st ed.

ISBN: 978-1-7367991-0-9

CONTENTS

INTRODUCTION

I am going to get right to the point. There is one thing that you truly need in this life, and everything else is secondary.

I am sure you can sense it. Have you been struggling in your relationships, but no matter what you do, you just can't find the kind of harmony you desire? Do you have constant anxiety or lingering questions about whether or not there is something more to this life? Do you wonder what will happen after you die?

Perhaps you know there is a God, but you do not know how to reach him. Or, you wonder if he hears you when you try to pray. Maybe you are afraid to approach him, because you are sure he is mad at you because of all of your mistakes.

Do you desperately want to be made right with God but don't know where to start? Do you see Christians who seem to have more peace and a stronger faith than you and wonder how they got it?

If you can relate to any of these questions, this book is for you. That one thing you need is Jesus, and understanding his message and how to have a relationship with him, as well as the peace that he offers, is not as complicated as it may seem at first.

You do not have to go to a Bible college or be a pastor to have a strong faith and understand the core message of the Bible.

I wrote this book for those thinking, *I want real faith and peace, but I have no idea where to start,* or those wondering if this Christianity thing is for real and how it can actually help them.

It began as a series of sermons, and I adapted it into a book to make it easy to talk about the concepts in a group or to quickly review topics you want to go over again.

Feel free to underline, circle or make notes all over it. Do whatever it takes so that in the end, you know exactly why Jesus died for you and how his message can totally, radically change your life.

CHAPTER ONE

YOU NEVER OUTGROW YOUR NEED FOR THE GOSPEL

T his book was written to give you the very basics, the fundamentals of the Christian faith. I will start by explaining the word *gospel,* and to set that up, let's talk about type one diabetes.

It is often called juvenile diabetes, because most people who have it are diagnosed at a young age. According to the Mayo Clinic, about 200,000 children a year are diagnosed with juvenile diabetes, and it is also referred to as "insulin-dependent" diabetes.

But type two diabetes is different. Usually you get it later in life. People with type two diabetes must be really careful about what they eat, how much they eat and when they eat, but with type one diabetes, you are dependent on insulin for the rest of your life.

Many years ago, if you were diagnosed with type one diabetes, it very well might have killed you, because we did not understand how the pancreas works or how it produces a hormone that makes it possible for cells to absorb sugar.

Now, let me explain why I am using diabetes to describe the gospel at the beginning of this book: If you have type one diabetes, you will be dependent on insulin for the rest of your life. It does not matter how much you eat, when you eat or what you eat... For the rest of your life, you are going to need the help of insulin to keep you alive.

There is no cure. There is no prevention. If you have type one diabetes, you are going to have it until your dying breath.

According to the Bible, we all have a type-one need. We all need the gospel of the Lord Jesus Christ for life! You never outgrow it. You never move beyond the need to be renewed by Christ. You never become Christian enough or read the Bible often enough to reach the point where you do not need the gospel of the Lord Jesus Christ.

Just like a type-one diabetic needs insulin with him or her for life, we never graduate from learning how much we need the gospel.

We never graduate from learning how much we need the gospel.
-Jeff Struecker
#startherebook

Caution: I am going to give a disclaimer about what I am going to say next about the gospel. For some people, what the Bible says on this subject is going to hurt a little bit. We are going to take a couple of key passages from the Bible, and it might sound like this is personally directed toward you. Just hang with me.

The word *gospel*, translated into the English language, means good news. The gospel is the good news that God has done something on your behalf to rescue you from the spiritual condition you are going to read about. And God continues to rescue you.

This need for the gospel is going to sound like a lot of bad news up front, but the good news only makes sense when you understand it in context to the bad news. When you understand how bad the situation is, the news does not just sound good; it sounds great! In the following chapters, we are going to unpack just how great this news is.

Spiritually Worthless

Let's talk about *why* we never graduate. Here is the first thing I want you to understand. (I am including me in this sentence, because it is true of everyone.) Without the gospel, we are all spiritually *worthless*.

I realize that word hurts. Bear with me for just a second. I did not make this word up. This is not the word I would choose to start the discussion about the gospel with; this is God's word to describe the spiritual condition of people who have not been made new by the gospel. This word comes directly out of the book of Jeremiah. In this passage, the prophet Jeremiah describes every human being on the planet, including me, as a sinner in need of the gospel.

Jeremiah 2:5-8 *This is what the Lord says: What fault did your ancestors find in me that they went so far from me, followed worthless idols, and became worthless themselves? They stopped asking, "Where is the Lord who brought us from the land of Egypt, who led us through the wilderness, through a land of deserts and ravines, through a land of drought and darkness, a land no one traveled through and where no one lived?" I brought you to a fertile land to eat its fruit and bounty, but after you entered, you defiled my land; you made my inheritance detestable. The priests quit asking, "Where is the Lord?" The experts in the law no longer knew me, and the rulers rebelled against me. The prophets prophesied by Baal and followed useless idols.*

Jeremiah is describing what it was like when God's people got to the point where they felt like they did not need him anymore. They thought in their hearts, *You know what? I'm good. I don't need God anymore. I am just going to take care of myself. I've got everything I need.*

And God, speaking to his people through Jeremiah, uses the words *useless* and *worthless*. Does the word worthless hurt a little bit? When I read this passage, it hurts me a little bit to hear it. It makes me want to say, "Wait a second, God. I'm not useless. I'm not worthless. There is some good stuff I can do. So when you say useless and worthless, that just doesn't sound accurate to me."

The Bible is not describing a person's physical, mental or emotional condition in this passage. Jeremiah is using language to describe people at the *spiritual* level. In fact, the Bible talks more about the spiritual side of a person than the physical, emotional or intellectual. And what God is saying is that all human beings (that includes everyone) have become worthless, or useless, because of sin.

Here is why God uses the word worthless. You were created in the image of God. When he originally made our first parents, Adam and Eve, he made those parents to represent him. In theological terms, the Latin phrase here is the *Imago Dei*, the image of God. What the Bible describes in Genesis 1 and 2 is God creating people to be his representatives. People were created to be morally pure. We were supposed to be morally perfect, but sin destroyed our moral perfection.

Every person who has ever lived since Adam and Eve, except for the Lord Jesus Christ, has followed in their footsteps and committed sin. And now that you have sinned, you are no longer pure. You are no longer 100% perfect.

No human being is crazy enough to say, "I am perfect, always have been, never messed up." When you made that first mistake, you were no longer worthy to represent God like he created human beings to represent him. This is why Jeremiah is using this painful word *worthless* to describe us.

I was struggling with a way to describe the significance of this word. I wanted a description that would help the reader understand what it is like to be a worthless representation of the image of God.

So, I thought about my cell phone. *-like when your cell phone breaks and the screen is cracked or when it's not doing what it's supposed to do...* But that does not really fit the word worthless, because even when my phone is not doing what it is supposed to, it still does some things right. It just doesn't do *everything* right.

So here is a better image: Imagine that you bought a bottle of very expensive perfume or cologne on Amazon. When the package was in shipping, the delivery guy started kicking it down the street, and the perfume shattered inside the package and spilled inside the box.

Now when you open the box, you have nothing but broken glass and this overwhelming scent of perfume or cologne. The bottle and package are *worthless*. You cannot do anything with them.

You cannot fix the broken bottle. The best you could do is rub the cardboard across your body (which I don't recommend) because this package is worthless. It cannot be fixed. It must be completely replaced.

That is the spiritual condition that God is describing in Jeremiah 2. God's word for mankind because of sin is *worthless*. That is the bad news. The good news is that Jesus Christ gave his life to save sinners. Spiritually, all of us became worthless after that first sin, but we CAN be made worthy again.

Spiritually Helpless

Look at what the Bible says next. Matthew 9 tells us that without the gospel, not only are we worthless, but we are all spiritually *helpless*. The word helpless means unable to do anything personally to fix our condition.

There are a few basic physical needs that every human being has. We have the need for food, shelter, clothing and water. Here, God is speaking to humanity through his son, Jesus (Matthew 9), and he is addressing how helpless we are spiritually.

You can do some things to change your physical condition. You can get some food to satisfy your hunger, and you can build a shelter to protect yourself from the elements. But spiritually, you are absolutely helpless.

Matthew 9:36 says it this way, and I intentionally used the *New Revised Standard Version* here[1]:

Matthew 9:36 (NRSV) *When he saw the crowds, he had compassion for them, because they were harassed and helpless, like sheep without a shepherd.*

Your Bible may use the phrase *distressed* or *dejected* or some variation of those two words to describe the sheep in this verse. Those are good words for what the Bible is saying here. But the *New Revised Standard Version* uses the word *helpless*. It is saying we are unable, incapable of fixing our spiritual condition.

I told you that the news is bad, and you cannot make it better.

So, the Bible makes this amazing statement that, "When Jesus saw the crowds of people like this, he felt compassion for them." Here is what this word *compassion* means. The Bible word compassion is referring to a physical reaction to the emotional or spiritual condition that Jesus sees.

In fact, if you have been heartbroken or have been through a breakup, you may have used physical language to talk about your emotions. We say that "our heart is breaking". It is not really breaking, but this is our way of describing how badly it hurts. Or, my friends and I would use the language, "This was like a punch in the gut," when something really bad happens.

The Bible is literally saying that Jesus just went through something like a punch in the gut when he saw the crowd's spiritual condition, because the people were helpless and could not fix their own spirits. Jesus has compassion for them.

Now, this crowd can get food. They can find clothing. They can build shelter. But, they cannot fix their spiritual condition. They are helpless without the gospel.

A long time ago, I used to teach ROTC students at the University of Louisville. I put a sign on the door outside of my office that was just a conversation starter. I will tell you; this sign got a lot of conversation. It had the recycle symbol on it, and then I wrote, "Jesus recycles people."

I wanted those college students to understand that when you finish using a plastic bottle or an aluminum can, you throw it in the recycling bin. That can is worthless and helpless to fix itself. It has to go through a very painful process in order for an old plastic bottle to become a new plastic bottle or an old can to become a new can.

That is why Jesus uses the language in John 3 of being "born again". You and I were helpless to be born the first time, and we are helpless to be born again.

I refer to this as the "miracle of new birth" because only God can make that kind of significant change in people. I put that sign on my door, because I wanted those college students to understand their spiritual condition is worthless and helpless apart from Jesus Christ. But with him, just like a plastic bottle or an aluminum can, he can radically, totally change us and make what was old and broken into something new and beautiful.

Picture in your mind who was in the crowd that day in Matthew 9. Just like today, there is no question there were some moms who were trying to take care of their kids. On the surface, it probably looked like they were able to keep everything going. But in reality, deep inside, they knew that they were barely hanging on to their marriages, and their families were just barely hanging together. They were terrified about how to face tomorrow.

In that crowd were likely some businessmen and businesswomen who had all of the nice clothes, and they were climbing up the corporate ladder. It looked like they had everything going for them. But deep inside, they knew they were shallow, and something was missing. They just didn't know what it was.

When Jesus had compassion on that crowd, there were probably some students who were dealing with all of the temptations that goes along with being in that kind of environment. - the sexual temptation, the substance abuse temptation, even the selfishness or the self-sufficiency temptation. Jesus sees this crowd, and he knows they are helpless; they cannot fix themselves.

Jesus's heart is broken because he knows, from way back in Genesis 1, this is not what he made people to be like. They are not supposed to be like this. And the Son of God has compassion on them. How much compassion? He decides, *I will do what it takes to rescue them. I will give my life in their place.*

Spiritually Lifeless

Without the gospel of the Lord Jesus Christ, all of us are also spiritually lifeless. This whole chapter is designed to talk to two categories of people. I am talking to the person who does not understand the gospel or has never embraced faith in Jesus Christ.

But I am also writing to the person who went through a religious ceremony a long time ago when they were a little girl or a little boy, and then somehow, some way, they got themselves to a point where they started to act like they don't need Jesus anymore.

Do you know we have a word for people like that? We call them *hypocrites*, because all of us need Jesus all of the time. We never get to the point where we are no longer type-one-dependent on Jesus.

Here is what Ephesians says about our spiritual condition before God steps in and does a miracle. You cannot miss the first few words stating that we were lifeless.

Ephesians 2:1-3 *And you were dead in your trespasses and sins in which you previously walked according to the ways of this world, according to the ruler of the power of the air, the spirit now working in the disobedient. We too all previously lived among them in our fleshly desires, carrying out the inclinations of our flesh and thoughts, and we were by nature children under wrath as the others were also.*

The Bible goes from bad to worse in Ephesians 2. Without Jesus, we are spiritually lifeless. I like Ephesians 2 because there is no mincing words here. Dead equals dead. You cannot do anything to bring life back to a dead person... but God can. The same power that raised Jesus up from the dead also jump-starts a dead soul and makes it alive through faith in Jesus Christ.

That same power sustains the human soul and keeps us going every day, longing for and looking for the grace of God and the gospel to change us today more than it changed us yesterday. That is why when I get up in the morning (I hope you feel the same way), I get up and make a simple prayer to the Lord:

"God, here I am again. You know what a mess I made yesterday. And God, without your strength, without your help, without your ability, I am going to make a big mess today, too. I need your gospel today as much as I needed it on the first day of my Christian journey."

I need you to understand something about the guy who wrote Ephesians 2. His name used to be Saul. He was a Pharisee, which is one of the most religious people on the planet. If there was a guy who knew all the right answers to all of the reli-

gious questions, Saul the Pharisee did... until he started traveling down a road to Damascus one day, and Jesus met him and
radically changed him.

That is the moment when Saul the Pharisee became Paul
the Apostle who writes Ephesians 2. That is the moment when
Saul realizes, "All of my religious efforts do not change the fact
that I am still dead on the inside."

This is Saul's "I saw the light" experience. We get this
phrase from what happened to this extremely religious man who
knew all the right answers but was still dead on the inside,
which means being religious and knowing the right answers
does not make you alive at the soul level. New birth is a miracle
that only God can do.

Saul became radically different when Jesus met him on a
desert road a long time ago. That is Saul's story. But Ephesians 2
is my story also. We are all spiritually dead. Even religion itself
is dead. All it can do is point out the bad we do. It cannot fix us
and make us do good.

The gospel produces life. Religion points to death.

Paul is describing how God jumpstarted his soul and
made a dead soul alive for the first time. Jesus alone can radically, totally change your life. He can change you from the inside-
out, also.

I was reading not long ago about missionaries in the
African country of Kenya. These missionaries were introducing
people to Jesus. Men's and women's lives were being changed.

Some of them were becoming church leaders and being called to start churches.

One Kenyan pastor who understood what the gospel does at the soul level started to look around his country. These are his own words to describe Kenyan Christians in 2018.

He said, "As I look at my country, about 80% of my brothers and sisters of the entire country of Kenya would call themselves Christian. They went down an aisle. They prayed a prayer. Maybe they even went through some religious ceremony that somebody told them was baptism. And then they just never, ever walked back into the doors of a church again. Nothing about their life changed."

Ken Mbugua, the Kenyan missionary, continued, "Most of them, by every measure that the Bible uses, could not possibly be considered Christian." And then he says, "The problem is that as I try to talk to them about Jesus, they quickly answer, 'I don't need it. I'm good because I did what a priest or the preacher told me to do a long time ago. So I'm already a Christian.' And then they go right back to living the exact same life that they've always lived."

Then Ken said, "This is my problem: How do you help people understand that they need the gospel and that they need church when they think they are already a Christian?"[2]

I want you to understand how the gospel fundamentally changes a person and how it causes a dead soul to become alive for the first time. If you have never really experienced this radical change, I want you to have that kind of experience. However, I am also writing to people who feel like they have gotten to the point where they do not need the gospel anymore. There is something broken with the idea that you do not need the gospel for the rest of your life.

A preacher in North Carolina by the name of J.D. Greear once said it this way, and he is absolutely right: "The gospel of the Lord Jesus Christ, his death for your sins, his resurrection, as the promise of eternal life is not the diving board that we jump off of and into the pool of faith; the gospel is the pool itself. We need that gospel every day, all day long for the rest of our lives."[3]

Here is the point that I am trying to make: All humanity needs the gospel. People outside of the faith need the gospel as the first step. It is the "start here" step of the Christian faith. But even those of us who have known Jesus for 30 years need the gospel as much today as we did on that first day. All humanity needs the gospel all of the time.

Apart from Jesus, we are worthless. Apart from what Jesus did for us on the cross, we are helpless. Apart from the resurrection that raised that dead man to life again, we are lifeless.

Going Deeper

1. Have you ever purchased a completely worthless product? How disappointed were you with it? What did you do with it?

2. When have you been the most helpless in your adult life?

3. Who or what do you feel the most compassion toward right now? Have you had the chance to put action toward your compassion?

4. Is there a group or a crowd of people that you think is more in need of the gospel than others?

5. In your own words, describe how the gospel changes a person.

6. What do you think it would take in order for a person to no longer need the gospel?

7. Pray for the Holy Spirit to show us our need for the gospel.

CHAPTER TWO

THE GOSPEL IS THE 4-LANE BRIDGE TO GOD

I do not always accurately define the word *gospel*. When preachers describe this word, they sometimes give you the short version, which unfortunately does not give the full meaning of this very important word.

It is like when you ask somebody to describe what it's like to be in love. When a teenager asks 50 people, "How do you know that you're in love?", they are likely to get 50 different answers. How can there be 50 different answers to one question?

Because this is such a powerful human emotion, when you put all 50 different answers together, it probably gives you an accurate picture of what it looks like to be in love.

This is also true of the word *gospel*. When you ask 50 preachers, "What is the gospel?", you are going to get 50 slightly different (or perhaps even significantly different) answers. And it is not that 49 of them are wrong. These 50 slightly different answers result from not giving the full definition of this word. So, in this chapter, I am going to try to give you the full of definition of the word.

Here is what I want you to understand about the word *gospel*: The gospel in one simple sentence is like a 4-lane bridge to God. I had an image in my mind of a 4-lane bridge to Heaven. But the problem with that imagery is, it does not describe what the gospel does for a human being today, right here on planet Earth.

You see, the gospel is all about life. It is about eternal life in Heaven. But it is also about abundant life here on Earth.

Thus, I am not only talking about a bridge that gets you into Heaven. Yes, that is a big part of the gospel. What I am really describing is a bridge that connects sinful people to a holy God, a bridge that would be so long that there is no way you could swim the distance between you and God on your own.

I want you to imagine the Pacific Ocean is the distance between a holy God and sinful people (It is actually far greater than the width of the Pacific Ocean, but work with me here). You are going to need a bridge, a 4-lane bridge, to help you get from where you are right now to the kind of person God created you to be. Two lanes of this bridge head toward God. The other two lanes, like any good 4-lane highway, head in the opposite direction, toward mankind.

Lane 1: We Get God's Love

Lane One of the gospel bridge is how sinful people get God's love. By this I mean to suggest that we all get something we do not deserve. Perhaps one of the most simple verses in the entire Bible to understand this lane of the bridge is Romans 5:8.

Rom 5:8 *But God proves his own love for us in that while we were still sinners, Christ died for us.*

Notice the word *proves*. This word describes God making something for a specific purpose. When you bake a cake, you bake it for a very specific purpose. Or when you build something in the wood shop, you build it with a purpose in mind.

We have all been burned by someone in the past. Guys, you maybe have had a lady who just took you for your money. She said she loved you, but she really just loved your money. Or Ladies, perhaps you had a guy who was only interested in your body. He said he loved you, but in reality, your body was all he really cared about. God says, "I will *prove* how much I love you. It is not about your money or your body. I will prove how much you mean to me."

Pay close attention to the timing in Romans 5:8: When you were at your absolute worst, when you were still in the middle of your sin, Christ chased after you, called you out of your sin and paid the ultimate price for you. He did this so that you could get a relationship with God that you and I do not deserve. He went after you to woo you and to pay your sin debt.

The timing goes like this: God did something for you when you were at your farthest point from him. When you were at your worst point, your lowest moments of your life, is when Jesus crossed the bridge to get you.

Think about it like this: You have been waiting for the next gaming console to come out, but you know you do not have the money to pay for it when it drops. You spend months waiting and longing for something you cannot afford. Then, all of a sudden, that console shows up on your doorstep, paid in full! That is what God did while you were still in your sins.

The gospel has nothing to do with you cleaning yourself up and becoming a good person. I want you to remember that when you were at your worst, when you were in need the most, that is when God showed up and showed his love for you. Lane One in this 4-lane gospel bridge is you getting God's love.

Lane 2: Jesus Gets God's Wrath

In Lane One, you get something you do not deserve, but in lane two, Jesus gets something *he* does not deserve. Jesus gets the wrath of God. What we deserve for our sins from Lane One, Jesus takes on himself in Lane Two. This is part of the definition of *gospel* that preachers (including me) often overlook. You see, we are really good (this is just human nature) at making the gospel all about us by only thinking about it from our perspective.

It is like a coin. A coin has two sides: a head side and a tail side. On the head side of this coin, we get God's love. On the tail side of the coin, somebody else has to take the wrath of God in order for that to happen.

I refer to this as "the great exchange." Jesus gets something in this great exchange that he does not deserve. He gets what *I* deserve.

I want you to see the great exchange in the words of 1 Thessalonians. Here, the Apostle Paul defines the gospel by describing what happened to us and what happened to Jesus in the great exchange.

> *1 These 5:9-10 For God did not appoint us to wrath, but to obtain salvation through our Lord Jesus Christ, 10 who died for us, so that whether we are awake or asleep, we may live together with him.*

Verse nine describes *how* we have been saved from the wrath of God. Verse ten describes *what it took* for us to be saved from the wrath of God. Verse nine is our side of the coin; verse ten is Jesus's side of the coin.

This passage is from a letter written to people who are wondering, "What happens to you after you die? Hey Paul, what is it like?" He answers, "Well, we Christians don't really die, but rather fall asleep. Christians are in the grave, but sleeping." They are *resting in peace*. But they will wake one day. And when they awaken, they will get the eternal reward of Heaven.

For us who are still awake, that reward starts right here, right now, today in the abundant life. We are able to experience the love of God, because Jesus has paid the atoning sacrifice for our sins. Through the gospel, we get abundant life now and eternal life after we fall asleep. That is what is waiting for God's people who have gone through the great exchange and received the gospel of the Lord Jesus Christ.

Now, when I use the word *wrath*, it may offend some of you. So I want to tell you a quick Bible story. In fact, I am going to give you a verse from the Bible to back this story up. One day, Jesus was walking with his disciples and like a classic helicopter mom, James and John's mother shows up. She pushes Jesus in a corner and says, "Hey Jesus, when you get to Heaven, because I love my boys and I know you love my boys, I want you to give them the best seats in Heaven with you."

In Matthew 20:22, Jesus responds by looking at James and John rather than their mother and asks, "Do you really want what your mother is asking for?" They shyly and sheepishly nod their heads and say, "Yes Jesus. We would really like to have the best seats in Heaven with you."

Then Jesus asks them a powerful question, "Okay, if you really want the best seats in Heaven, are you able to drink from the cup that I am about to drink?" Without even thinking about it, they shoot their mouths off and say, "Of course, Jesus. We are ready to drink the cup that you are about to drink" (because they have no idea what is in the cup to which he is referring).

They should know what is in the cup, because the Bible references it in Job and Isaiah. But perhaps the clearest reference that Jesus is making to the cup of God's wrath is found in the book of Jeremiah. Here is what Jesus is saying is about to happen to him in order for us to get God's love:

> *Jer 25:15-16 Take this cup of the wine of wrath from my hand and make all the nations to whom I am sending you drink from it. 16 They will drink, stagger, and go out of their minds because of the sword I am sending among them."*

When Jesus answers James and John's mother and says, "Do you really know what you are asking?" he looks over at these two disciples and says, "Do you have any idea what it is going to take for me to make people right with God?" They have no clue, but they quickly answer, "Yes Jesus, whatever it is, we are willing to go through it with you."

He says, "Oh no. You do not have the first idea what you are getting into, because in order for sinful people to be made right with a holy God, I am going to have to drink the full measure of God's wrath." Jeremiah describes it like staggering drunk under the brutal force of the wrath.

In Lane Two of the gospel bridge, Jesus endures the full weight of God's wrath so that you and I can be made clean in his sight. We preachers sometimes forget to describe the gospel in terms of what it cost Jesus.

That is why Communion is so important to the Christian church. During this holy ordinance, we remember Jesus's broken body. We think about his blood poured out so we can be made right with a holy God.

Lane 3: Jesus Gives His Righteousness

In Lane Three of the gospel bridge, Jesus gives something away. He gives away his righteousness. Now, theologians refer to this concept as *imputed righteousness*. Let me explain what imputed righteousness looks like when we get something that we did not do anything to earn. This is found in 2 Corinthians:

> *2 Cor 5:21 He made the one who did not know sin to be sin for us, so that in him we might become the righteousness of God.*

The pronoun *he* in this verse refers to God. Jesus took upon himself our sins, and God held Jesus accountable for our mistakes and failures. This verse is saying that we get credit for something that we did not deserve; we get put into our account a credit for something that we did not do right. On this lane of the gospel bridge, God deposits into our bank account a paycheck we did not work for.

I want you to think about it like you are on a softball team, and the softball team has one win and 20 losses. You see, what preachers often do is treat the gospel like it is just wiping the losses off the books. Jesus's blood pays for your sins. This is absolutely true… It is just not the whole picture. The other half of the picture is getting *credit* for something you did not do.

Recently, I was meeting with a couple, and I had the privilege of sharing the gospel with them. I asked them, "What do you think it takes to get into Heaven?"

One of them basically answered, "I think by being a good person and my good deeds outweighing my bad deeds, I will get into Heaven."

I tried to explain, "I don't think you really understand how sin works, nor the moral perfection that God expects of people." If the gospel were just God wiping the losses from your softball team off of the books, your team would have a record of one and zero, one win and zero losses. The 20 losses just went away, but we do not get credit for any wins. Forgiveness of sin alone makes us morally neutral in the sight of God.

The other half of the gospel, the other side of the coin, is that God now gives us credit for something we did not do. He says, "Not only am I going to wipe those 20 losses off the books, but I am going to put wins in their place. I am not giving you credit for a win because *you* did anything right, but because of what my son Jesus did right. Because of the righteousness of my son, Jesus, I am going to now make your record 21 and zero. I have just changed your 20 losses to 20 wins."

Through Jesus's imputed righteousness we get something we did not work for and credit for something we do not deserve. And we get credit for the good deeds that Jesus accomplished. This is what it looks like to have the righteousness of God "credited into our bank account", according to 2 Corinthians 5:21.

Here is how I ended my conversation with that young couple: "When you and I stand before a holy God, he is not going to see Jeff's mistakes (though there are lots of mistakes that I deserve to pay eternal punishment for). God is not going to see those mistakes because they were wiped off of the books by the blood of Jesus Christ". Jesus's imputed righteousness will do the same for you also.

So far we have covered three lanes on this bridge. We have seen that we *don't get* something that we do deserve in Lane One, we *get* something that we don't deserve in lane three, and Jesus *gets* something that he doesn't deserve in lane two when he takes on himself the wrath of God. (Remember, two lane head toward God, and two lanes toward mankind on this bridge.)

In Lane Four, Jesus *gives* something. We get his reward when we stand before God in Heaven. This is where the whole gospel picture starts to come together. Jesus gives us credit for what he did right.

Lane 4: We Get Jesus's Reward

The first part of Ephesians 2 shows how sinners are lifeless and totally dead apart from the gospel of the Lord Jesus Christ. But when you get to verses eight, nine and ten, the Bible makes it abundantly clear that nobody can take credit for what happens inside of us.

> *Eph 2:8-10* *For you are saved by grace through faith, and this is not from yourselves; it is God's gift—9 not from works, so that no one can boast. 10 For we are his workmanship, created in Christ Jesus for good works, which God prepared ahead of time for us to do.*

There is no way, looking inside us, for salvation according to these verses. You and I cannot take credit for the good gifts that God gives us. According to the gospel, you do not have to bear the responsibility for all of the bad you did. However, you also cannot earn God's favor by being a good person because the system does not work that way.

The Bible leaves no room for confusion. The gospel is all about the work of the Lord Jesus Christ on our behalf. The gospel is all about what he did for us. The wrath that he took on himself now makes it possible for us to be made right with God in Heaven.

This four-lane bridge we are seeing in Ephesians 2, in Romans, in Thessalonians and Corinthians shows how we can be reconciled to God. Ephesians says that no human being on the planet could cross the gap between sinful people and a holy God.

So, God takes the initiative, and God goes after sinful people. He cleans us up and makes it possible for us to be made pure, holy and righteous in his sight. And he does it through the sacrificial death of his son, Jesus Christ.

I was thinking about what a good modern-day example of this would be like. Frankly, I could not find one. There are some pretty amazing bridges out there that span some pretty impressive distances, but none of those bridges really describe what it would look like, what it took, in order for you and me to be made right with God.

I instead went to one of the epic fiction books of the English language, *The Lord of The Rings* written by J.R.R Tolkien. Tolkien wrote this series of books to describe the gospel. He wrote the books to represent Jesus Christ and to show how far apart sinful people are from a holy God.

In the first book, *The Fellowship of The Ring*, this little band of misfits is trying to do away with the temptation destroying the world. In order to do that, they have to go return back to the source. They have to go back and throw away the ring of power.

On their way, they are going through the Mines of Moria. Tolkien describes a moment where they have to cross a bridge. In fact, he gives this bridge a name: Khazad-dum. They are being chased by the enemy who will do whatever he has to do to destroy them, and he sends one of his greatest monsters after them, a Balrog called Durin Bane. The bridge represents temptation, struggle and suffering on one side, and it represents safety and the way to Heaven on the other side.

If you have ever seen the movie, *The Lord of The Rings: The Fellowship of The Rings,* there is this epic show down on that bridge. In order for the fellowship to be healthy, safe and successful, the wizard Gandalf is going to have to sacrifice himself.

There is this great gap between who we were created to be and what sin did to us. Because of sin, we are no longer acceptable in the sight of God because we are broken, stained, marred images of what God created us to be. If we were to try to fix this on our own, it would be like trying to swim from Sydney, Australia to Seattle, Washington. It is humanly impossible. No one can pull this one off because God's standard for Heaven is moral perfection.

So, through the gospel, God created a bridge between his holiness and our sinfulness in order for us to be made pure in his sight. God cleanses our sins and we get credit for what Jesus did for us. But Jesus had to pay the price, the ultimate price.

The word *gospel* can be defined by just four words: Jesus gives; we get.

We give nothing, yet we get everything. Jesus gives everything so that we can get his righteousness and his reward. When a Christian stands before God in Heaven, God looks at him or her and sees the good works of his Son. He gives us credit for what Jesus did. Not only that, but he gives us this abundant, everlasting, eternal life. And it starts right here, right now on planet Earth.

Going Deeper

1. "How do you know when you are in love?" (How would you answer this question to a teenager?)

2. What is the most favorable trade you have ever made?

3. In your own words, define the gospel.

4. At a minimum, what do you think a person must understand in order to understand the gospel?

5. Has anyone ever stepped in and taken the blame or punishment for something you did wrong? If so, when?

6. Do you believe someone can understand the four lanes of the gospel but still not be a Christian? If so, how?

7. Pray for the gospel to soften the hard times and make the good times greater.

CHAPTER THREE

WHAT IT COSTS YOU TO FOLLOW JESUS

I want you to imagine that you are sitting down at a restaurant having a conversation with a friend who has been thinking about the Christian faith. In this conversation, your friend has heard what you have said about the gospel (that it is a four-lane bridge (refer to Chapter Two of this book), and now your friend has started to understand the basics of the faith.

Picture in your mind that this person then asks you a really raw, really honest question. "I think I understand what you're saying about the Christian faith and the definition of the word *gospel*. But I just need to know something right up front. Before I step across the line of faith, before I take that final step, I need you to look me in the eyes and tell me... what is this going to cost me?"

Few people ever get the chance to ask a question like that out loud. Maybe they are embarrassed or do not know anybody who could give them an honest answer to that question. That is tragic, because this question is extremely important. It is the kind of thing that you would want to know before you sign the mortgage on a house. You would want to know this before you agree to a job.

You would want to know this before you go deep in a relationship with a guy or a girl. You would want to know, *what is this going to cost me?* And I think people absolutely should be able to ask the question about following Jesus.

How would you answer that question? What would you say if somebody asked you to look him or her in the eyes and tell them exactly what this is going to cost?

I believe in truth in advertising about the Christian faith. Therefore, I think we must give an honest answer to this question. Here it is:

Following Jesus will cost you less than you think and more than you can imagine.

–Jeff Struecker
#startherebook

By the time you finish this book, if you properly understand the gospel, hopefully you will have decided, *I am willing to give everything that it costs me, because I believe I am going to get a whole lot more out of it than I will give up to follow Jesus.*

I believe this one question has two answers to it. It may seem weird at first, like "Wait a second. This isn't fair. You can't give two seemingly contradictory answers to the same question." Bear with me; these answers are not contradictory. They are actually complimentary. And these two complimentary answers are a really honest picture of what it costs to follow Jesus.

So, we are going to take both sides of this equation in this chapter and look at the three things it is going to cost you, as well as three things it will *NOT* cost you.

It Will Cost the Shame

First, it is going to cost you some shame over the mistakes you have made in your life. Now, if you are like me, you have done some things in your past that you are not proud of (by the way, I don't even need to know you to know this is true of you). If you say, "Hey, I've never messed up or made a mistake," then I am going to call you out on it right now for lying, because we all do it.

Unfortunately, your past mistakes can haunt you into the future. Did you know that the gospel says you do not have to carry the pain of those mistakes or the shame of those mistakes with you into the future?

The prophet Isaiah many hundreds of years ago was writing to God's people. They had made some massive mistakes. They had committed some sins that were so bad, God sent a foreign army in to conquer their land and took them away into captivity.

God was restoring the land and through his prophet, Isaiah, he was promising a future where his people would not have to carry the shame of their past mistakes with them. I want you to hear what Isaiah chapter 54 says about how God's glorious gospel does away with this shame.

Is 54:4. *"Do not be afraid, for you will not be put to shame; don't be humiliated, for you will not be disgraced. For you will forget the shame of your youth, and you will no longer remember the disgrace of your widowhood."*

When Isaiah is writing this, he is describing what we may call today a modern-day "Karen". I was scrolling through *Apple News*, and I stumbled across a headline that said, "Help! My Wife Made a 'Karen Video' on Social Media."

I do not spend a lot of time on social media. So, I did not have the first idea what a "Karen video" is. I had to go do a little bit of research about this. This title is referring to "Karen" as a stereotype. If you do not know what this term means, "Karen" is a middle-aged, affluent white woman, usually with a bob hair-cut, probably a racist, who does something that she is ashamed of, and that thing makes it to social media.

In this *Apple News* article, the wife did something and had a meltdown in public. Her husband was writing to try to get some help because his wife had become a recluse and refused to go out of her house. Now, please pay attention to the pain this family was experiencing. The wife herself admitted, "I have just said something that I am so ashamed of that I don't even want to leave my house." And the family was asking the question, *is it time for us to move*? That is how bad life has become for this family when the wife's actions went public.

When you ask the internet for an answer, you are going to get some crazy opinions. Some people replied that it was time to move and start all over again. Others said, "Here's how you pick up the pieces after you have done something that you're personally embarrassed about." The husband was not embarrassed for his wife; he was saying, "My wife is so embarrassed that she has become a recluse."

I wish somebody on that forum would have given the answer that this guy and his family really needed to hear. It is a two-word answer: *the gospel.* The gospel is the solution to the shame of a mistake that you have made in the past that continues to keep up with you and haunt you. Isaiah's explanation of the gospel means, "You do not have to let your past mistakes and failures define who you are today, nor do they have to go with you into the future."

God is saying, "I will take all of those mistakes, all of those sins, all of those failures, and I will erase them." Then you can get up in the morning and not feel the shame of those major mistakes you made in the past.

It Will Cost the Pain

You are going to give up your shame when you commit to Jesus. And by the way, most of us would say, "I'm more than willing to give that away." Here is what else the gospel will cost you: You are also going to give away some of the pain that life inflicts when it punches you in the face and kicks you while you are down.

I want to point you to Psalm 25, but before we get there, I need you to understand that the Bible never promises God will prevent you from having pain. In fact, in this earthly city in which we live, the Bible almost guarantees that some painful times will come.

But, it also says that there is an eternal city waiting for us when God will do away with all of the suffering, all of the tears, all of the pain. In Psalm 25 we see that he promises he will walk with you through the pain.

It hurts, but it does not hurt nearly as badly, because you have the Holy Spirit of the living God going with you in the midst of some intense pain and difficult problems. Five times in Psalms 25, David cries out for God to make the pain go away, or at least, "God, be with me in the midst of this pain." Here is what he says:

Ps 25:16–20 (NLT) Turn to me and have mercy, for I am alone and in deep distress. 17 My problems go from bad to worse. Oh, save me from them all! 18 Feel my pain and see my trouble. Forgive all my sins. 19 See how many enemies I have and how viciously they hate me! 20 Protect me! Rescue my life from them! Do not let me be disgraced, for in you I take refuge.

Maybe you feel like David right now, and maybe life has punched you and kicked you while you were down. Maybe you have had some people turn on you and stab you in the back. The guy who writes this Psalm knows what it feels like to be in pain. We do not know exactly what is going on in his life, but maybe this is the time when has a father-in-law who will do anything to prevent David from taking the throne, to include killing him. His own father-in-law wants him dead.

Or maybe it is even worse than that. Maybe it is the moment when David's family falls apart, and he is experiencing the pain of his son sleeping with David's wives and trying to murder him because he wants his dad's job, power and wealth. Maybe that is what is going on when David cries out to God, "God, I am hurting!"

And what he says here is, "I just need to know that you feel my pain. I just need to know that you will walk with me [Psalm 23] through the Valley of the Shadow of Death. I just need to know that you are going to be by my side." David is hurting, and he is turning to a God, who is present and walking with him through the midst of the pain.

Recently, a friend named Elspeth shared her faith with a sales associate while shopping. She was at a clothing store when she asked this worker for help. It was obvious that this lady serving her was in deep distress and really troubled.

So, Elspeth took a courageous step and just simply started a gospel conversation. During the conversation she learned: This young, 21-years-old lady was now pregnant with her second child, and her family did not know yet. She was experiencing the pain and the shame of having to go tell her family that she was now pregnant with child number two and not married.

I am so proud of Elspeth when she simply said, "The answer to your shame, the answer to the pain that you are going through is found in King Jesus." And although Jesus did not save this woman right there on the spot, the sales associate just reached out to her and said, "Is it okay if I give you a hug?" And that hug meant so much to her, that Elspeth got emotional.

Maybe the emotion was because of the struggles she saw this woman going through. Whatever it was, what this sales associate just needed to know was that there is somebody who cares about her and who would go through this pain with her. That is what David is saying.

It Will Cost the Strain

Following Jesus is going to cost you shame over some mistakes that you have made in the past. It is going to cost you some of the pain that life has inflicted on you. And finally, it is going to cost you the strain of trying to work your way into Heaven.

I was a chaplain on active duty in the United States Army in the the 82nd Airborne Division when the attacks on September 11, 2001 happened. The men in my unit, the paratroopers in the 82nd Airborne Division, were struggling and stressed out. They were thinking through the impact that these attacks were going to have on them, their families, and on our country.

My commander gathered the entire unit together and just basically gave them some remarks on what he thought the future would look like. I asked my commander at that time, "Do you mind if I read one or two verses from the Bible and just say a quick prayer over all of these paratroopers?" I wanted to offer some peace in the midsts of an uncertain future.

The verses I wanted these paratroopers to hear came from Psalm 46, because when you are struggling and suffering, when you are really having a hard time, I believe you need to remember how big our God is. Psalm 46 ends this way:

Ps 46:10–11 *"Stop fighting, and know that I am God, exalted among the nations, exalted on the earth." ¹¹ The Lord of Armies is with us; the God of Jacob is our stronghold.*

And then he says the word *Selah*. The idea behind the word *fighting* here (depending on your Bible translation; it may also say *cease striving)* is swimming in the ocean as hard as you can. The current is stronger than you can swim, and you are fighting against the current with every ounce of energy. However, no matter how hard you swim, you do not get closer to shore. You just keep getting pulled farther and farther away.

The Bible recognizes that sometimes you will struggling in life. Sometimes it feels like *no matter how much I give, no matter how hard I try, I just keep getting pulled further and further away. Life feels like I take two steps forward and three steps back. And at the end of the day, I'm further than I was when it started.*

Maybe that is what life feels like for you right now. When you turn things over to Jesus, the Bible says you have a God who is bigger than your problems, a God who is bigger than the warring factions on Earth, bigger than even the chaos and the 20 years of combat that the global war on terrorism started.

What I wanted these paratroopers to hear is how great our God is and to put their trust in him and only in him.

Are you struggling right now? Are you suffering? Are you feeling like the deck is stacked against you and that you cannot get ahead? If that is you, stop fighting. If you have gone through some shame and made some mistakes in your past and they are haunting you today, stop letting that shame define who you are in the future.

If you are struggling with some really difficult, painful circumstances, turn those things over to Jesus, and he will help you through those problems. That is what following Jesus is going to cost you.

But, I also want to tell you, the second half of the equation. I want you to also know what it is NOT going to cost you. I want you to understand what changes when you become a follower of Jesus and what *doesn't* change.

It Will Not Cost Your Brain

Let's transition the conversation and look at the three parts of this equation that do not change when you become a follower of Jesus. First, you do not have to check your brain at the door. It will *not* cost you your intellect. Someone recently asked the question, almost exactly in these words: "I don't feel like I have enough faith to take this blind leap. And so, I guess I'm just not going to become a Christian."

The idea behind this question is, "I've been thinking about it, and the math doesn't add up."

I just want you to hear what the Bible says, because one of the most brilliant minds on planet Earth had this radical experience with Jesus Christ that changed him completely. He also realized, *I don't have to check my brain at the door. I don't have to give up my intellect. I can really think through what I believe is a reasonable faith.*

This comes from the Apostle Paul, and it is found in 1 Corinthians. See how he describes following Jesus in this short verse.

1 Co 13:12 For now we see only a reflection as in a mirror, but then face to face. Now I know in part, but then I will know fully, as I am fully known.

I want you to understand that the Christian faith is a reasonable faith. Now, let me explain the word *faith*. Ultimately, it is a belief. Nobody can believe for you. Nobody can take that last step of faith for you. You are going to have to do that one on your own.

Nobody can twist your arm into believing something about Jesus. I called it a reasonable faith, because if you look at the history, if you look at the archeology, if you look at the ethics behind it, if you look at theology, if you look at the evidence in the Bible, when you look at all of these things together, it becomes *highly* reasonable to believe the claims of the Bible makes about Jesus.

It is reasonable to believe that there really was a man who lived 2,000 years ago who claimed to be the Son of God, to believe that he said he would become the lamb of God who takes away the sins of the world, and that he died a brutal death by a Roman cross, to believe that they took a body off of the cross (a man who really was dead) and then three days later he came out of the tomb by his own power and is alive today and at the right hand of God, the Father.

I cannot conclusively prove these things to you, but when you look at all of the evidence, it becomes highly reasonable to believe that what the Bible claims about Jesus really did happen. Now, the way the Apostle Paul said it in 1 Corinthians is that faith is like looking through a mirror. You are just seeing a reflection right now.

He says we are looking through the eyes of faith at a God that we cannot see. We are looking through the mirror of faith. But there will be a point in the future when faith becomes sight and where I see with my eyes what I have believed with my heart for a lifetime.

I just want you to understand that it is really reasonable. You do not have to take some blind leap that defies logic. No, the last step of faith should make sense. The evidence points the way to taking the last step of faith and surrendering control of your life to Jesus. It is highly reasonable to believe the claims of Jesus. It is rational to believe he is who he said he is and what he did for you. You do not have to forfeit your brain to become a Christian.

It Will Not Cost Your Campaign

I wish I did not have to make this next statement, but unfortunately, I do. You also do not have to give up your *politics*. Because I was looking for words that rhyme, I just used the word *campaign*. But somebody asked me this question: "When you become a Christian, can you really vote for a political party that endorses abortion and basically treats moral injustice like it's no big deal?"

Now, I want to give grace to the person who asked this question. I hope he or she was genuinely looking for an answer rather than trying to endorse one political party over another.

Every four years, our country is torn at the seams by two political parties, and my answer to the question, *do you have to become a a member of a certain political party when you follow Jesus?* is a resounding... No!

In Luke 6 we learn about the kind of people Jesus asked to follow him. I want you to understand something about the last guy listed in the long list of 12 apostles.

Luke 6:13; 15 *When daylight came, he summoned his disciples, and he chose twelve of them, whom he also named apostles:*v *14 ... and Simon called the Zealot*

Now, there were two Simons whom Jesus called to be his apostles. One of them, Jesus changed his name and called him Simon Peter. The other Simon, the Bible refers to as Simon the Zealot. Are you aware that "Zealot" is a reference to politics?

There was a political party in Jesus's day of fierce nationalists who believed the nation of Israel should violently rise up against all foreigners in their land. Eventually, years after Simon lived, the Zealots would try to violently overthrow the Roman government. They attempted to kick the foreigners out of Israel. Simon was a Zealot when Jesus called him to become his disciple.

Notice, the Bible does not say that he had to give up being a Zealot to follow Jesus. I think his politics probably shifted over time, but Jesus intentionally went after Simon the Zealot.

Now, I am not comparing either political party in the United States to the Zealots. I think this verse implies that Christians are free to vote for whatever political party that most honors God. I get very angry when I hear Christians cheapen the gospel by attaching it to a certain political party.

Do not cherry-pick political issues with me. It is not going to end well. Taking one political issue and making that one equal with the gospel is a sin. I do not look to the government to fix the problems of our society. I believe only King Jesus can fix the ultimate problems in our society. Understand the issues. Know who the candidates are and what they stand for, and vote your conscience before a holy God.

Yes, there are some issues that should significantly influence the way we vote, but we vote our conscience before a holy God. What politics has done to our country, especially the two-party political system, is abhorrent to me. It is shameful. And unfortunately, it is causing division in the church. Shame on us if we allow politics to ever become more important than the gospel!

The President of the United States cannot change a someone's soul. Only King Jesus can do that, and only by changing souls will society ultimately change.

It Will Not Cost Your Name

Third, someone also has asked me the question, "Where do Christian names come from? When I become a Christian, does the Bible necessarily say that my name has to change?" This question asks, does everything about my past, my identity, my characteristics, the things that were unique to me, do those things go away when I become a Christian?

The gospel will not cause you to change your name. You see, the things that were true about you (your height, the family you were born into, your hair color), all of those things are still true after Jesus saves you.

God changes people from the inside out. In Genesis chapter 17, God did something in Abram's life and changed his name to Abraham. But all of those things that made Abraham who he was remained the same. God just took those things and molded and forged them into the character of a man different on the inside, not on the outside.

Gen 17:3–5 Then Abram fell facedown and God spoke with him: 4 "As for me, here is my covenant with you: You will become the father of many nations. 5 Your name will no longer be Abram; your name will be Abraham, for I will make you the father of many nations.

Back in Old Testament times, names often referred to the character that parents wanted their son or daughter to possess. Parents generally gave names based on what they wanted their child to become one day.

But the family characteristics, the person you were and the environment that you grew up in, those things do not change. God cleans up the messes that we were raised in. He redeems our background and makes it beautiful. He makes something beautiful out of ashes. He restores what the locust has eaten. He makes all things beautiful in his own time.

Abram had some family problems. God said, "Abram, I am going to change you from the inside out. Those family problems are still there, but now I am going to make you into a new man. And this new man will become the father of many nations. By the way, the name *Abraham* is a reference to your new future as the father of many nations."

My first sermon I ever preached to an army chapel audience was in Fort Knox, Kentucky, in 1999. I was a chaplain candidate working in a basic training battalion, asked to preach a chapel service in a little small army chapel that really seated about 150 people. I am not making preacher exaggerations with these numbers. There were probably more than 200 guys in the room that day, because they were standing in the aisles, in the back of the room, by the stage, and every seat was full.

I do not even remember the text, but I presented the gospel. I asked the men in the room who understood the gospel and were ready for Jesus to change them, to come forward. No exaggeration; more than 50 guys in the room got up, started to move forward and flooded the stage. It scared me; it freaked me out. I thought, *Oh no! I've said or done something wrong.*

So I told them, "Stop. Go back to your seats, and sit back down again. I'm not sure what you just heard. I'm not even sure what I just said, but it doesn't sound like you understood what I was saying. I can't get you out of basic training. If you feel like you made a mistake and you want to go home, that's not what this is about. If you really, genuinely want Jesus to change you and to clean you up on the inside, then I'm going to invite you to get back up again and to come forward." And still about 30 guys came forward. True story.

So I sent them back to their seats and made one more statement. I said, "Guys, let me make sure you understand what you're doing next. If you are saying, 'Jesus, I will go anywhere. I will do anything. I will give up whatever it is that you have ask me to give up; I will give it all up to follow you,' then I'm inviting you to get up one last time and to come forward." About 15 guys got up and came forward.

You see, at the beginning I think what a lot of those guys were interested in was some "get out of Hell; I just don't want to have to suffer the consequences of my sins" faith. And what they heard from me was not the whole story. So I needed them to hear the whole picture. Following Jesus will cost you more than you can possibly imagine, but it will also cost you less than you think.

I had the privilege of following up with those 15 guys and seeing them go through baptism. I believe that those 15 guys are genuinely followers of Jesus Christ today.

Maybe today is the day that you need to take this final step of faith. This step will cost you more than you can image, but less than you believe.

Going Deeper

1. What is different about you since following Jesus?

2. Does *believe* mean that you cannot also have evidence for the Christian faith?

3. Describe a painful moment from your past. Has Jesus helped you deal with that pain? (If so, how?)

4. How do you normally respond after you have done something for which you are ashamed?

5. What is the appropriate level of trust Christians should place in politics or government?

6. Is there an area of your life that is causing you great stress right now?

7. Pray for the Holy Spirit to change you or continue to change you into the image of Christ.

CHAPTER FOUR

LIFE'S GREATEST TREASURE

If you think about it for a moment (and you do not have to think very hard), you would have to say that the greatest treasures on Earth cannot be purchased with money. In fact, some of the most important and most priceless things in our lives, money did not buy. They came from relationships, time and hard work.

One of Hollywood's biggest stars was an actress named Judy Garland. If you saw the movie with Renee Zellweger called *Judy,* you have seen what a huge star she was. For 45 years, Garland was one of the mega-stars of Hollywood. She was the original star from *A Star Is Born*. Long before Lady Gaga and Bette Midler, Judy Garland was the star in the movie, *A Star Is Born.*

Maybe you do not recognize any of the old black and white movies she was in, but you probably saw the movie *The Wizard of Oz*. Garland played Dorothy, and it was one of her most famous roles. Judy Garland had all of the fame, all of the money and all of the celebrity status that the world had to offer. But she used to tell people that all of that stuff does not really satisfy you deep inside.

In fact, she said, "The greatest treasures are those that are invisible to the eye, but are found in the heart."

I want to take what Judy Garland said and ask you, how do you get those greatest treasures? What do you use to buy the greatest treasures in the world?

Here is what I want you to understand: Life's greatest treasures, because they are priceless and because you cannot use money to buy them, are really bought with the currency of your heart.

Life's greatest treasure is bought with the currency of the heart.
-Jeff Struecker
#startherebook

I want you to picture in your mind that you are living in Bible times. Imagine Jesus comes to your town, looks you in the eye and tells you the same thing that he told all of his disciples. He points straight at you and says, "Come and follow me."

Now, you are going to have two natural questions for Jesus. The first question is going to be, "What do I have to give up if I follow you, Jesus?" That is a good question and a natural one. We answered that question in the last chapter.

The second question that is going to be on your mind (and don't act super spiritual like you're not going to think along these lines, because even the apostles asked this question) is, "What do I get out of it, Jesus? If I give up what you're asking me to give up, what do I get out of this?"

You see, sometimes when Jesus asked people to follow him, they could see the treasure, the priceless treasure that they would get out of it. They left their nets and families, and they immediately followed him. Sometimes, though, Jesus called people to follow him, and those people thought about all that it was going to cost them, and they turned around and walked away.

The Bible says that Jesus felt compassion for them. His heart broke for them, because they were not able to see the priceless treasure that Jesus was offering. In the Bible book of Matthew, there are two really short stories. Actually, they are so short that these two stories only take up three verses in the Bible. In these three verses, Jesus describes what you gain by following Him.

Mt 13:44–46 *"The kingdom of heaven is like treasure, buried in a field, that a man found and reburied. Then in his joy he goes and sells everything he has and buys that field. 45 "Again, the kingdom of heaven is like a merchant in search of fine pearls. 46 When he found one priceless pearl, he went and sold everything he had and bought it. [Emphasis added]*

Jesus describes three priceless treasures that come with a relationship with him, and I want you to see what you get when you follow Jesus.

Jesus Gives Joy

The first thing is, Jesus gives unimaginable joy. Now, I want you to work really hard not to compare and contrast these two stories. I am the kind of guy who will nerd out on the details in the Bible. And sometimes by doing that, I focus so much on the trees that I miss the whole forest. I think by focusing on the similarities and differences of these two stores, you can miss out on the big picture.

If we were to take a step back and look at both of these stories, it is pretty easy to see that Jesus is trying to communicate something to us, something really important, in both of these stories.

By the way, did you know that sometimes Jesus uses two stories back-to-back, telling the exact same thing, just to drive a point home?

By the time you get to chapter 13 in Matthew, five times Jesus has talked about the Kingdom of Heaven and what it is like. One time he used two back-to-back stories, the story of the mustard seed and the story of the yeast, to demonstrate what this is like.

When he gives two back-to-back stories, this is a really, really important point that Jesus does not want his people to miss. So, he starts to describe for us this joy that someone finds in following him.

Imagine that you are going to an estate auction, and they are selling the furniture, the drapes, the house and the car. Basically, most of the possessions are up for sale.

Now imagine that you are at the estate auction, and of course, the auctioneer is bringing things across the auction block. The pictures, the drapes, and the furniture, that stuff is just natural. You would expect that to be sold at an auction. But this auction gets a little bit weird for you because what the auctioneer brings across the auction block next is the cleaning items from underneath the kitchen sink that have probably been there for years.

Then the clothes go across. And pretty soon it gets really weird because now the auctioneer is selling off the condiments from the refrigerator. He is selling the mustard and the ketchup… everything. Everything is up for sale!

You would look around if you were one of the bidders and say, "What on earth is going on?" But wait. It gets weirder, because imagine that on the stage in a chair next to the auctioneer is the person selling everything.

Usually estate auctions are for when somebody dies and the family is getting rid of all of the possessions. But picture in your mind that the person selling everything is on stage, and when the favorite family portrait goes up for sale, that person is not miserable. He is actually smiling when the auctioneer hammers the gavel down. When the clothes, the cars and the furniture go up for sale, the smile gets bigger and bigger on that person's face. You would start to ask the question, "What has gotten into him?"

And if you were in the crowd the day that Jesus told this story, you would stand there and scratch your head saying, "Why would this person be willing to give all of this stuff up?"

What Jesus is trying to explain to us is, the person selling all of this at auction is going to gain a lot more than he is going to give. He is going to receive a whole lot more than he is going to have to release. In his story, this guy is walking across the field, stumbles on treasure that is priceless, and says, "Of course I'll sell everything I own, even the clothes on my back, to go get *that* kind of treasure."

When I say Jesus gives joy, I am using a different idea of joy than most people have.

I am not talking about the temporary happiness that goes with buying a new car, and when the new car smell is gone, so is the happiness. I am not talking about standing in line for days to get a coupon for Chick-fil-A for a year, or about waiting for a brand new iPhone.

All of the kind of joy that goes along with that junk erodes. No, when Jesus gives joy, he gives eternal, permanent joy. He gives a kind of joy that lasts for a lifetime, and quite literally, beyond.

When you realize this the kind of joy that Jesus gives, you are more than willing to make the sacrifice. I am more than willing to give up whatever it is going to cost me next, because I believe I am going to gain a whole lot more than I give up. That kind of joy permeates deep in the soul, and it goes on in eternity. Even after the body wastes away on Earth, that joy lasts for eternity. When Jesus gives joy, he is giving *his* joy. And *his* joy is eternal. *His* joy is permanent.

That is why this guy is willing to sell everything and be happy. He enjoys selling everything, because he realizes what he gains is far greater than what he gives up.

Jesus Gives Peace

Jesus not only gives joy, but he also gives peace. Now, I need to explain to you that the peace Jesus gives is a deep-seated, bigger-than-circumstances peace. I am not saying that you will not have problems; I am saying that you will have peace in the midst of problems. Jesus gives peace that is permanent.

Ultimately, all problems are temporary, because there really is an eternity waiting for all human beings, an eternity with God in Heaven or eternity in Hell separated from him. When Jesus gives a priceless treasure, part of that treasure is harmony and peace with him.

It is actually more than that, though. It is peace with others and peace even with nature itself. This guy that Jesus describes, the jeweler, or the merchant in verse 46, the language that Jesus is using suggests this guy has been on a journey and has been looking for something.

You can imagine the anxiety, struggle and searching that have been going on, because he probably understands how precious jewels are. He has been longing for and looking for the perfect pearl. In verse 46, Jesus says, "When he found the perfect pearl, he was more than willing to go sell everything and to go buy that perfect pearl."

It was because this guy had been looking for and longing for something. And now he had finally found it. Everybody on the planet was created with a similar longing inside them. This spiritual void that we all have can only be filled by an intimate relationship with God.

Jesus is describing what it is like when things are finally settled between you and the God of the universe with this story. Maybe this guy has been searching for a lifetime, and when he finally finds the perfect pearl, this jeweler is happy to sell it all because he realizes, *that* pearl it worth much more than the asking price. It is of infinite value, and whatever they ask for it, the jeweler is willing pay it because it is worth a whole lot more than the price tag on it.

When I was studying, I came across a quote by Mother Teresa. Now, you probably recognize this Catholic nun who served her entire life in some of the most miserable conditions on Earth. She helped orphans who were living in Calcutta, India, and she saw intense suffering and great pain.

People would travel from all over the world to come to her orphanage in Calcutta, and when they asked her about the struggles, the war, the violence and the difficulties in the world, Mother Teresa made this statement: "If we have no peace, it's because we've forgotten that we belong to each other. And because we forgot we belong to each other, we start to go to war with each other."[6]

I am telling you, if you look at what is happening, not just in America, but all over the world, if you look at the political division, the racism and social upheaval all over the world today, every one of those things is a result of a lack of peace.

There is something missing in people's hearts, and they are struggling to find it. This is the root source for racism, political division, broken relationship and war.

I was recently traveling to the west coast of the United States. All the time, there are wildfires consuming hundreds of thousands of acres of land. At the time, there was smoke covering 1,000 miles of territory; the entire state of Washington was covered in smoke.

The news reports were blaming a couple that did a gender reveal party, and that party led to fires, which ultimately cost dozens of people their lives.

Did you know the wildfires in California, the suffering in Calcutta, hurricanes, tornadoes, earthquakes and war all have a common starting point? All of these ultimately began back in the Garden of Eden.

When God created human beings, the Earth he created was a perfect paradise. Man was in perfect harmony with nature, in perfect harmony with mankind, and man was in perfect harmony with God. When our first parents, Adam and Eve, committed that first sin in the Garden of Eden, it immediately affected their relationship with God. Since then, every person is longing for peace.

The first sin immediately affected Adam's relationship with Eve. Suddenly, those two did not have the perfect marriage anymore. It affected their relationship with nature because God says in Genesis 3 that even the earth itself will now be cursed.

Wildfires, earthquakes and war ultimately point back to the peace that was broken at the Garden of Eden. Jesus came to Earth to restore peace, to give us peace between men, peace between man and nature, and peace between man and God. Only Jesus can give that kind of peace. That is the peace that all human beings are longing for deep inside their souls. And Jesus is the only solution, the only answer, to that kind of longing.

Jesus Gives Fulfillment

There is one more priceless treasure that I want you to hear about from Matthew 13. We have already seen that Jesus gives joy. We have seen that Jesus gives peace. But at its root, ultimately what Jesus gives is fulfillment. You see, this farmer is looking for something, and he finds a treasure. When he finds that treasure, he finds what he has been looking for. Maybe a better word than *fulfillment* is the word *wholeness*.

When this jeweler is searching, the idea here is this jeweler has been looking for a lifetime and finally finds the perfect pearl. When he finds it, he is now whole and fulfilled on the inside.

And of course this farmer is going to buy that field. Of course the jeweler is going to buy that pearl, because the jeweler knows, "I am getting much more than I am giving here." The farmer knows, "I am receiving a whole lot more than I am paying. This field is worth much more than I'm paying for it because of what's buried in that field."

The fulfillment that these two guys find in the Bible for the first time perhaps in a lifetime is a deep satisfaction on the inside. You probably heard when you were growing up, "You can't grasp and take hold of something that somebody is offering to you when your hand is full, or clenched."

If you really want what Jesus is giving, when he gives joy, peace and fulfillment, the only way to receive that is to let go of what you are currently clinging to. And the thing in your hand that I am talking about, the thing that I think Jesus is trying to point to, is control over your life.

The only way that things are really going to change is when you radically and totally surrender control to Jesus and say, "Jesus, I'm going to give it all over to you. And in exchange, I'm asking for something in return. I am shamelessly like the apostles asking, 'What do I get out of it?'"

These two stories in Matthew 13 demonstrate the reward of a life surrendered to King Jesus. His peace sustains you, even in the midst of terrible problems. He gives the soul-level satisfaction of knowing that Jesus has everything under control. Jesus settles your anxiety and offers what you are longing for.

Ultimately, what Jesus asks everyone to do is to step across the line of faith and to make a choice. The choice is to either hang on to control and you continue to call the shots in your life or give control away to Jesus. When you give Jesus control, you get joy, peace and fulfillment in return.

Most Bible scholars will tell you that if you really study and nerd out on this passage, ultimately it is really talking about God, who is the jeweler in this story. He is looking for the perfect pearl, and you are the pearl! So God decides, "I want that pearl, and I'm willing to give up everything (including my son) in order to get it."

You are the pearl. In order to buy us back from our sin and clean us up to make us holy, God gives everything. In a suicide mission on the cross to purchase you back from your sins, God is willing to go to that extreme.

In return, he radically and totally changes people and gives them joy, peace and fulfillment on the inside. It is God who does the sacrificing, and all that he asks you in return is to simply give away control of your life to him.

Put it all in his hands. Trust his Holy Spirit, and follow him for a lifetime. He will do incredible things in your life.

Going Deeper

1. Is there a difference between "joy" and "happiness"?

2. For what purchase have you worked the hardest and saved the longest?

3. What is your definition of "peace"?

4. What brings you the most joy in life right now? How has this area of your life changed over time?

5. Where do you think most people turn for peace in their lives? Why?

6. Read Psalm 38:9. What do you think is the deepest desire of most people?

7. Pray for peace with God and with other people.

CHAPTER FIVE

THE GOSPEL CHANGES THESE 3 RELATIONSHIPS

To review where we have been so far, Chapter One answered the questions, what does this word *gospel* really mean? Chapter Two explained why everyone on the planet need the gospel. In Chapter Three, we got real with each other and answered the question, what is it going to cost me if I respond to the gospel and give my life to Jesus? Then, Chapter Four answered, what do I get in return?

In this final chapter, we are going to answer what I think is probably one of the most important questions about the gospel. "How *exactly* does believing the gospel change me? I know it's supposed to make things different, but what is different, and how exactly does it make things different? If I believe what the Bible says, what does that do inside of me?"

In order to set this up, we are going to look at just three verses in the Bible. But first, let's just talk about social distancing. All of humanity, everybody on the planet, has gone through some form of social distancing during the coronavirus outbreak. For most of us, social distancing is really difficult. I am one of those guys who really likes to give a guy a handshake or give a lady a side hug sometimes.

This two meters of separation that the world went through is really difficult on a lot of people. Maybe you are feeling close in the heart, but distant physically to someone right now. Or, maybe you felt distant in the heart, as well.

Here is the overarching answer to the question, how exactly does the gospel change me?

The gospel changes you in such a way that you never have to be two meters apart again.

–Jeff Struecker
#startherebook

There are three relationships that are radically, fundamentally changed by the gospel, and all three of these relationships are found in 2 Corinthians 5. I want you to hear the gospel in a nutshell from 2 Corinthians 5.

2 Cor 5:17–19 Therefore, if anyone is in Christ, he is a new creation; the old has passed away, and see, the new has come! 18 Everything is from God, who has reconciled us to himself through Christ and has given us the ministry of reconciliation. 19 That is, in Christ, God was reconciling the world to himself, not counting their trespasses against them, and he has committed the message of reconciliation to us.

How many times in this passage do you see the word *reconciled* or some version of it? It is four times in two verses,

(18 and 19) that this word shows up. So, it is probably a really important concept.

Jesus Fixes Your Relationship With God

The first change that the gospel makes is like the super-glue that fixes relationships. It fixes all relationships. It closes the two-meter gap, and it makes us intimate again. The number one relationship is your relationship with God. When this relationship starts to get fixed, all others start to fall into place.

Let's do a little Bible word study on *reconciled.* because I do not want you to miss its significance. There is something broken in our relationship between us and God. That gap is much bigger than two meters.

Think about it like the distance between Earth and the moon. Even further than that is how far sinful man is from a perfect, holy God. So God takes the initiative and closes the gap. He is perfect, and we are sick. He comes to sinful men and women to rescue us, to clean us up, and to fix our relationship with him.

The Bible word *reconcile* appears more than 1,500 times. Usually the word refers to others (the other team, the other people, the other town). That is how this word is almost always used in the Bible. But there are six places where a variation of this word is used.

It is used very differently from all of those other hundreds of times here. I rarely do this, but it is the Bible word *katallassō*. This word is used once in the book of Romans, once in 1 Corinthians, and *four* times in the verses that we just read. It is the only time this word is used this way in the Bible. What this word is really describing is an enemy!

Now, you are probably thinking right now, *"Wait a second, Jeff. Are you saying that God considers me his enemy? I don't have anything against Jesus. I think Jesus is a pretty cool guy. I am just busy and don't spend my time reading the Bible. I don't spend my time going to church. I don't spend all of my time praying. But that doesn't mean that I'm the enemy of Jesus."*

If that describes you, then you are an enemy of God. The Bible make is clear that there can only be one person who has first place in your life. When you take first place of your own life, this is called idolatry, and idolatry is worshiping self instead of Jesus. This is exactly the kind of person that the Bible is talking about in 2 Corinthians 5. The enemy of God is not just somebody who is doing something because he or she hates God. It is somebody who just has placed himself or herself in God's position.

The Bible is saying that God took the initiative to reconcile his enemies, to clean them up and to bring them into a relationship with himself. Now, you are no longer his enemy. Now you have become his friend. Or a better description would be God's son or daughter.

Let's use American baseball as an example. Baseball in America is basically just like cricket… except totally different. There is a bat and a ball. Actually, that is about the only thing the same with American baseball and cricket.

In American baseball, you have two leagues, and these two leagues play baseball very differently from one another. The two are the American League and the National League. In one league, the pitcher has to hit the ball (this is real baseball), and in the other league, he doesn't.

Let's say you live in Chicago. There are two teams from the two different leagues: the Chicago White Sox and the Chicago Cubs. Nobody in the city of Chicago cheers for both the Cubs and the White Sox. You can root for one or the other, but you do not cheer for both of them.

In American baseball, the teams play in their leagues until you get to the number one team in the American League playing against the number one team in the National League in what is called the World Series. It is a best-of-seven series.

The Bible describes embracing the gospel as a radical change in your life. It would be like a player going from baseball for the Chicago White Sox to the Chicago Cubs in Game Two of the World Series! You totally switch teams, and now you are on the opposite team. This is what the word *reconcile* means. It is switching from your team to God's team in the middle of the championship game.

It is God going after enemies, recruiting them to play on his team and calling them sons and daughters. It would be like somebody leaving his team to go to play for the opposite team in the world championship of baseball. That is how big of a deal this change is that the writer of 2 Corinthians is trying to describe for us.

I went through a change like this, and many of you have, too. Wherever you are, whatever your past, he can radically, completely change you, and now you are no longer on the opposite team. Now he has called you into a relationship with himself and because that relationship has changed, it also changes your relationship with other people.

Jesus Fixes Your Relationship With Others

Let's just be honest; all of us (I don't need to know who you are or where you live) have "people problems". These people problems are part of the human condition, and because the gospel fixes our relationship with God, now it starts to work on us, and it starts to fix our relationship with other people.

I literally do not know a boss who has not said, "The most difficult challenges that I deal with are people problems. I would rather lose a million dollars in revenue than have to deal with people problems at work, because these problems are difficult and heartbreaking."

Maybe you feel like you are going through those people problems right now. Maybe you live in the same home and sleep in the same bed, and although you are not six feet apart at home, your hearts are really halfway around the world from each other. The gospel is supposed to move in and make an impact on you. And because it starts to change you, it changes your relationship with other people.

Maybe a great way of describing the idea from 2 Corinthians is God cleaning people up. God cleans people up by making them new. God fixes broken relationships by re-creating people. Remember in Chapter Four, we talked about how this relationship problem between people started all the way back in Genesis 3?

When Adam and Eve sinned, they started to hide themselves from each other by sewing fig leaves together. If you read carefully from Genesis 3, what you will see is, Adam starts to point his finger at Eve. Eve starts to point her finger at somebody else and to blame these problems on him.

Go one chapter more in the Bible, and you will read about the first murder. Their son, Cain, kills his brother, Abel. That is how bad the people problems get because of sin. The gospel eradicates sin, which makes it possible for two broken people to become intimate with one another again. I am talking about problems at work, problems in school and problems at home. All of those problems can be fixed. They are all changed because of the gospel at work inside of you.

I received a letter from a guy in basic training. His first name is Joseph, and he asked a simple question. He said, "I'm a Christian. I just started basic training on Fort Benning, and I just want you to know it's absolutely terrible."

Now, basic training is supposed to be terrible. Basic combat training in the US Army, is supposed to be tough.

Here is what Joseph said next: "It's 11:14 at night. I'm on fire guard in the barracks in Fort Benning, and I don't know who to turn to. I found your booklet, *Bulletproof Faith*, with your address and Jeff, I have a question for you."

Now, I remember fire guard because I went to basic training on Fort Benning in wooden World War II barracks. It is the kind of building that if you drop a match, it is going to go up in flames in 30 seconds or less.

Now, Joseph is going to basic training in a barracks made out of wood, metal and brick. But you know military tradition. We are going to make you stay awake and watch for fire even though there is never going to be a fire in the room.

Here is what Joseph's letter said (exact words): "I'm trying to live out my faith. I'm trying, working hard to be [listen to these words] loving, patient, and kind [these are Bible words], but I am absolutely surrounded by people who are hateful and frustrating and full of negative, bad emotions."

His letter asks me, "How do you do this? How do you be kind and loving and patient when you're surrounded by negativity and hostility and bad emotions?" Great question, right?

I ordered a little book that I sent to Joseph in the mail, but there is a one-word answer to his question. It is the word *gospel*. Until the gospel changes the hearts of the people Joseph works with, it is *always* going to be a struggle. Until the gospel really gets to work in human relationships, there are always going to be problems. The gospel, and only the gospel, can fix the things that Joseph is dealing with.

My guess is, you are dealing with these problems where you work or where you live, too. The President of the United States cannot fix the people problems in America; only the gospel can. A Justice of the Supreme Court will not fix people problems. People problems exist in the heart. And until something changes the heart, nothing changes between people.

The writer of 2 Corinthians is telling us that your heart can be changed by the gospel. And the people you have problems with, their hearts can be changed by the gospel also. If this has never happened to you and your heart has never been changed before, let me know so I can talk to you about having this new creation, new birth, miracle of God, change your life.

Remember, we are answering the question, "How exactly does the gospel change me, Jeff?" Well, it changes your relationship with God, and it changes your relationship with others. But you might say, "Okay Jeff, wait a second. You are saying the gospel changes everything, but tomorrow when I get up, I will go to the same office and have to deal with the same boss. I am in the same classroom, and I have to put up with the same professor. I have to live in the same dorm with the same roommate. I have to spend my time around the same people. So you tell me, how exactly does it change *that*?"

Jesus Fixes Your Relationship With Self

Here is the answer to the question: The gospel changes everything, because the gospel changes *you!* It ultimately deals with you, and because *you* are different, every other relationship, every other circumstance, is now different as a result. What you have in 2 Corinthians 5:17 is a picture of God re-creating a new human being.

Verse 17 says that God created. What he created was pure and perfect. Then sin entered into the equation, and it destroyed the perfection that God created. As a result, God had to step in and do a miracle. This is the miracle of new creation, making something that was broken totally new again. He is not just talking about an upgraded version. He is talking about completely, totally new.

When the Bible says, "All things are being made new," it is going to affect your relationships at home, work, school, at play and every other relationship. This relationship impacts them all. If you are honest, you might say, "Man, I've made some mistakes in my past, and I wish those failures would go away!" The gospel, and the gospel alone, can fix those failures.

If you are saying, "Jeff, I've got some real struggles. There are some flaws that I know are inside of me, and I wish I could fix them. But try as hard as I might, I keep falling off the wagon. I keep going back to the same old sin. What can possibly fix me?", The gospel and the gospel alone can change that. It can change your frustrations. It can change your future. It changes everything because it changes *you*.

I am afraid some people read the Bible and go to church and miss the gospel completely. Perhaps the best way to describe it is, the gospel is like having eye surgery. Before eye surgery, you can see, but what you see is cloudy and dim. Then all of a sudden, God does a work, and he re-creates and fixes your eyesight. Now that you can see clearly, *everything* becomes clear.

What the gospel does is, it changes everything about you. It changes everything about the way you see the world. It changes all of you relationships. If the gospel has not made that kind of impact on you, perhaps you have never really believed the gospel. Maybe you have just accepted a set of Christian doctrines as true, but you have never really *embraced* the gospel. It makes a radical, total change in a human being.

Nobody had the right to say it more than the guy who wrote this passage. Do you remember Saul, who became Paul? Remember that he was a Pharisee, a religious leader who hated Christianity with a passion and was willing to do whatever he could to stop Christianity, to include killing Christians.

He was a first-century version of an ISIS terrorist. Saul the Pharisee was on a road to the capital city of Damascus, when Jesus met him and radically confronted him with the gospel. Then Saul the Pharisee changed so much that he became Paul the Missionary, perhaps one of the greatest spokesman for Christianity in all of human history apart from Jesus himself.

Multiple times, Paul would tell the story of that encounter with Jesus along the road. He used the language of being blind, blinded by the light. Then God cleared up that blinding, and he could now see.

The same gospel that radically changed Saul the Pharisee into Paul the Missionary and changed a 13-year-old kid like me, can change you.

If you have never really understood, never really accepted Christ, it was the broken body and the poured out blood of Jesus Christ that Paul had no answer for when he was confronted on the road to Damascus.

Going Deeper

1. Do you wish you had something new right now? If so, why?

2. What can people offer to our God (who is complete and perfect) in exchange for peace with him?

3. Why does it feel so good after a broken friendship or family relationship has been restored?

4. Give an example of what peace with God feels like.

5. What is one mistake that you wish you could go back and undo?

6. What is the most challenging relationship in your life right now?

7. Pray for the Holy Spirit to help you reconcile with God, others and self.

SUMMARY

In this book, my goal has been to give you a solid understanding of the gospel, which is the starting point of the Christian faith. It is the good news of Jesus Christ, the perfect Son of God, rescuing us, sinful people, who could not help ourselves. He offers himself in our place, and as a result, we can receive forgiveness, a new heart and eternal life!

In Chapter One, we talked about how without Jesus, we are spiritually worthless, hopeless and lifeless. He gives worth, hope and life, and no matter how old you get after making the decision to follow Jesus, you *always* need him every single day.

Chapter Two gave a more full understanding of the word *gospel* by using the imagery of a 4-lane bridge. In salvation, we receive what we do not deserve (Jesus's righteousness and rewards), but Jesus receives our punishment and takes what he does not deserve (the wrath of God) on our behalf.

In Chapter Three, we discussed what it will cost to follow Jesus. We learned that it will cost less than you think, but also more than you can imagine. I listed three things it *will* cost you, as well as three things it *will not* cost you. In following Jesus, you give up control of your life, but you receive far more than you give up.

Chapter Four then laid out the "treasures of the heart" that you receive through a life with Christ, namely indescribable joy, peace and fulfillment.

Finally, I ended with a chapter on relationships. Life is made up of relationships, and you know that those can be tricky sometimes. But, Jesus has the power to fix broken relationships by working on how you relate to him, others and yourself. If we will let him, he can literally transform us, which will affect all of our relationships.

If you know that the gospel and the restoration that Jesus can give you is what is missing in your life, I would like to pray for you. Email me at info@2citieschurch.com to let me know either that you would like prayer about this or that you have made the decision to follow Jesus. If that is the case, I would like to celebrate with you.

After reading about the starting point of the gospel, you probably have some follow-up questions, which is normal as you start this journey in the Christian faith. To help you get some of those answers right away, I have included a bonus section next, which gives answers to 33 of the most often asked questions about God, faith and the Bible. Many of them were asked during a question and answer series I did live online. Chances are, you are thinking about some of these very same questions.

REFERENCES

[1] *New Revised Standard Version Bible (NRSV)*: Harper One, 1989.

[2] Mbugua, Ken"Africa, the Prosperity Gospel, and the Problem of Un guarded Churches," *9Marks Journal, Spring–Fall, Special Edition* 4 (2018): 98.

[3] Greear, J.D., and Timothy Keller. *Gospel: Recovering the Power That Made Christianity Revolutionary.* B&H Books, 2011.

[4] Tolkien, J. R. R. *The Fellowship of the Ring: Being the First Part of The Lord of the Rings.* First published in Great Britain by George Allen & Unwin, 1954. Second edition 1966.

[5] Garland, Judy. https://www.inspiringquotes.us/author/4078-judy-gar land.

[6] Mother Teresa. https://www.brainyquote.com/quotes/mother_tere sa_107032

BONUS: Answers to 33 of the Most Asked Questions About God, Faith and the Bible

QUESTION #1: When people's names were changed in the Bible, is that a Bible way of describing them becoming a Christian? Also, is this where we get the phrase "Christian name" from?

I am going to answer the second question first, then I am going to go back and answer the first question. The answer to the second question is: no and yes. A Christian name actually comes from christening, which comes from the middle ages. Baptizing a baby, in some traditions, continues to this day. Today, Godparents present an infant to the parish priest using a "Christian name".

The term "Christian name" has also been used as a synonym for surname for many years. When filling out legal documents today, most will ask for your given name and surname. Before "given name" was a common phrase for your first name, the term "Christian name" was used as a legal way to identify you. In legal documents, your given name, or Christian name, didn't really have anything to do with christening or baptism. It was just another way to say "the name that you were given by your family".

But now let's go back to the first half of the question. It asks about God changing someone's name (e.g. from Abram to Abraham). Here is my answer: In Bible times, parents gave names not because they sounded cool, but because the name represented the character that they wanted that child to have. Often, when God changed the name of a person in the Bible, he was really saying, "Your character is changing, or your destiny or your future is changing." So you'll no longer be called Jacob, which is deceiver or trickster. Now your new name will be called Israel, Son of God.

The new name represented a new character of the person, but it also recognized a new parent, namely, God the Father changes the name of his son or daughter. This question is complex, and there is a lot more history involved in the answer than I have time to discuss here.

Here is one more quick thought about this question, though. If you become a believer in a foreign country where the majority religion is a pagan religion today, often you will take a Christian name. I believe the Christian name represents a change of identity and a change of relationship.

You were once an enemy of God. Now you are a son or daughter of God. However, to be honest, sometimes the Christian name is just so that people like me can pronounce your name. For native English speakers, the Christian name is sometimes much easier to say than the Chinese or Indian name given at birth.

QUESTION #2: What does Jesus's death have to do with me going to Heaven?

One word: Everything!

Now, I am going to give you a lot more detail than just one word. But the Bible uses the words *worthless (Jeremiah 2:5), useless (1 Peter 1:8), and lifeless (Ephesians 2:1)* or "dead" to refer to people apart from Jesus. These Bible words refer to people who have not been covered by his blood on the cross and been made alive with his resurrection power. So the truth is, without the cross of the Lord Jesus Christ, all of us, 100% of us, Romans 3:23 says, "Have sinned and fall short of the Glory of God."

All of us deserve death. All of us deserve Hell. And, all are spiritually dead until made alive by the sacrificial death of Jesus on the cross. According to the Bible, apart from the death and resurrection of Jesus Christ, no man, no woman, no matter how good, how godly, how hard they work, or how much religious effort they give, can be made right before God's sight. This is why nobody deserves to get into Heaven except through the death and resurrection of the Lord Jesus Christ.

QUESTION #3: If I am unworthy, why is God willing to give his son to rescue me?

Basically, this question can go in two different directions. If you go to the left, the question appears to ask, "Am I really unworthy of Heaven, Jeff? -because if I really am spiritually unworthy, why would God send Jesus to die in my place? Because God was willing to make that kind of sacrifice for me, maybe I am not really unworthy after all. I'm not perfect, but I'm pretty important. 'I'm a pretty big deal,' to quote Ron Burgundy in *Anchorman*."

But if you go to the right with the question, it appears to ask: "Wait a second. If I really believe what the Bible is saying, and the Bible really does use the word *dead* in Ephesians 2, *unworthy* in Jeremiah 2, and the word *useless* from the Gospels, then why would God do this? I believe what the Bible is saying, but now it doesn't make sense that God would do something like this for me."

I pose these left and right directions, because I want you to hear the powerful theology in this question. It gets to the essence of the gospel and asks, what prompted God to reach down into my sin and to save Jeff Struecker? What prompted him to send his son, Jesus, to go rescue you or me from sin, clean us up, and make us acceptable in God's sight? If I'm really dead/ unworthy / unable/ useless, why would God do something like that for me?

The reason why this question is so powerful is because it really helps us to understand the gospel. You really cannot understand the good news, if you don't recognize the corresponding bad news. I recently heard a very intelligent woman explain it this way: In order to understand this question, you really have to understand just how terrible sin is and just how offensive it is to a perfectly holy God.

Because sin is so terrible and so offensive, God cannot overlook it. His holiness and his justice won't allow him to blow off my sin. This is how the gospel puts God's justice, his holiness, his mercy and his love on display all at the same time.

I would add that God *chooses* to love people. There is nothing that I offer in this relationship. There is nothing that God needs from me that I can give him. He chooses to shower his people with love and with mercy.

If you really understand the bad news, the good news isn't just good; it's great (better than Tony the Tiger's GREAT)! It's almost indescribably great how good the good news is when we really understand the bad news.

I also want to add this. God does this for his own glory, and the Scriptures make this point over and over again. God shows his glory by taking the weak and making them strong, by taking the foolish and using the foolish to confound the wise.

He uses those that are nothing and makes something out of them so that we cannot possibly take credit (Ephesians 2:8-9). He acts so that when people see the difference in our lives, it points to God, not us.

I hope people don't say, "What a great change has happened in Jeff's life!" I would rather people say, "What a great God who could do something like this for him! And if God can do that for him, then maybe he can do that for me, too."

This is why the right side of the question is so powerful, "I think I believe what the Bible is saying, and if it's saying that I'm unworthy, I don't understand why God would do something like this."

If you are still struggling with the left side of the question, let's go back to the last question, because I am not sure you understand why Jesus died on the cross if you still think you are a pretty good person.

QUESTION #4: How can Christians say that their religion is the only true one?

I want to push back against this question. I am going to give an honest answer, because any time somebody asks an honest question, I believe he or she deserves an honest answer. But my struggle with this question is with the word *religion*, because technically speaking, Christianity does not claim to be a religion.

Most religions, at their essence, are faith systems that establish a set of rules. These rules, when properly observed, earn the religious follower favor from their deity. Christianity does not fit into this definition. In Christianity, the God of Heaven acts on behalf of people in rebellion.

The essence of Christianity is built on a foundation that God acts on behalf of fallen creatures to make them acceptable in his sight. The method whereby he does this is through the sacrificial death and bodily resurrection of his son, the Lord Jesus Christ. This distinction is how Christianity is fundamentally different from all other religions.

God's sacrifice of his son on behalf of sinners is proof that other religions cannot be true *along with* Christianity. If people were able to earn their way into Heaven by following other religions, then the death of Jesus Christ is unnecessary. Jesus's death and resurrection are proof that Christianity is the only true religion.

QUESTION #5: Do all religions lead to the same God?

The answer to this is a two-letter word: No.

Most Muslims would not say, "I worship the same god as the Jews." Nor would a Buddhist say, "I worship the same gods as a Daoist or Hindu." I do not know of any religion except universalism that says all religions lead to the same god. In fact, all religions are distinguished by what makes *their* god different from other gods.

Most pluralist religions, which follow many gods, would add another deity to their list to worship, but they do not really practice a faith that believes all gods are the same.

I was doing a television broadcast a few years ago. The interview was tape-delayed and broadcast early in the Global War on Terrorism. The reporter asked, "How can you Christians believe that your God is better than all of the other gods?"

I had to ask a clarifying question: "Are you asking if Christianity worships the same God as Islam? Because if that is what you are asking, I am sure your viewers would answer this question unequivocally, no! This is not the same God."

Any Christian should be able to easily answer, "What you are describing definitely does not fit the God of the Bible, who has chosen to reveal himself in the form of Jesus Christ, and who dwells inside of me as the Holy Spirit. No, that is not the same God as other religions."

QUESTION #6: Why do "religious" people seem to be the most judgmental people?

This question stings just a little bit, doesn't it? What hurts about that question is the fact that there is a lot of truth to it. I can only imagine how this feels to someone outside of the church. A judgmental attitude toward somebody outside the faith does nothing positive to help him or her understand the God of love and grace who was willing to sentence his son, Jesus, to die to make him or her holy.

I think there are some really cranky and uptight Christians out there, because they are trying to follow a set of rules. These people are breaking their backs trying to follow a set of rules because a pastor has turned a relationship with Christ into a dead religion by preaching a set of rules. I call these "Do this but don't do that" sermons.

And because they are breaking their backs trying to follow these rules, they get angry when they see other people who are not also breaking their backs trying to follow the same set of rules. And so, they then start to become highly critical and judgmental of everybody around them. Somehow, they stopped relying on the power of the Holy Spirit to live pure lives. Instead, they are trying to be righteous by their own power. It is oppressive, because you and I do not have the power to be righteous on our own. Only the Holy Spirit can live the life we see in the Bible.

In fact, this very judgmental attitude could be an indication of a spiritual pride that needs to be repented of. Now, I think when people properly understand what it took for God to rescue them, they want others to experience the same thing. And second, when you see a brother or when you see a person who is clearly in sin, struggling with a lifestyle that does not honor the Bible and does not honor our God, instead of criticizing that person or complaining about that lifestyle, we should have a heart that breaks for him or her. Like Jesus, we should have compassion and a broken heart for those who are wandering around like sheep without a shepherd.

Instead of pointing the finger, maybe what we should do is reach a hand out toward them, pray for them, and introduce them to our Savior. I hope you would not be considered among those religious people who are just cranky, critical or judgmental. I hope you are the kind of person who never washes over sin, while at the same time is willing to lend a hand and help a brother or sister who is obviously in sin.

Instead of addressing the sin before explaining the gospel, let's explain the gospel first and then talk about the sin later. However, when we talk about sin, it should be with love and with grace rather than criticism or judgment.

QUESTION #7: If I can't do any good works to get to Heaven, then why should I even try?

Let me just give you a very succinct Bible answer to this question. Good works, by God's definition, would be moral perfection in thoughts, attitudes, and actions. Let me make it more clear. Moral perfection means our thoughts, attitudes, and actions are perfectly in line with God's thoughts, God's attitudes, and God's actions. I do not know anybody who would say, "Yes, I am morally perfect."

I don't think most of us could say that we have been morally perfect even part of the time, if that is what moral perfection means. Most of us would have to say, "If moral perfection is measuring up to God's standards for thoughts, attitudes, and actions, then I am not sure I've ever done that." This is what the Bible means by "good works".

But the question asks, *why even try*? Perhaps that is how you feel now that you know what the Bible means by good works. Maybe you are thinking, "I can't be good enough to get into Heaven, so I am just going to throw my hands up in the air and go live however I want." If that is how you are feeling right now, let me remind you that the Holy Spirit gives God's people the power to live up to God's standards. So, you do not have to try. My advice would be to stop trying to be good, and allow the Holy Spirit to make you good enough.

If, however, what you mean is, "God knows me, God made me, and God knows that my works aren't good. So, I'm not even going to bother because God will just forgive me no matter what I do," That is a very different question.

A Christian lives in such a way to bring glory to God and honor to the name of Jesus, not to earn his approval. I cannot be morally perfect by my own effort. But, I can let the Holy Spirit work through me in such a way that it brings glory to God and does good for other people.

QUESTION #8: How can a loving God send people to Hell?

This question gets asked a lot. For people outside the faith, I think what they are saying is, "I'm struggling with the idea of God being loving and also sending people to Hell. If God was a really loving God, he wouldn't send people to Hell." For Jesus's followers, many are asking, "Why do people not embrace the faith? Why do people end up separated from God forever"? Depending on what angle you are looking from, this question can look very different.

Here is the really short, and I think equally challenging, answer to this question: God ultimately gives people, at their death, exactly what they have been asking for. Those who are apart from God, even though he has been drawing them to himself, even though many people have talked to them about Jesus, those who say, "I don't want Jesus. I don't want anything to do with God," when they die, they receive the consequences for that lifestyle.

So, you could almost say in answer to this question, that people send themselves to Hell. Now, of course, God is the ultimate judge. But it is not God's fault that they end up in Hell. Since God has done everything on our behalf necessary for someone to escape the punishment of Hell. It is because of a resistance or the refusal to accept God's gracious gift of salvation that they go to Hell.

For the Christian who is struggling with why anyone would ignore God's gracious gift of eternal life, the only answer possible is SIN. It has so blinded people that they cannot see the benefits of accepting God's offer of eternal salvation.

QUESTION #9: How can the Bible be trusted?

There are really two ways to answer this question, and both are appropriate. There is the external evidence and internal evidence. This is how Bible scholars, theologians, and Christians apologists (That word simply refers to people who defend the Christian faith) use two broad categories to answer this question.

External evidence is, let's look at the claims that the Bible makes and then let's look at the archeological evidence. Let's look at the scientific evidence. Let's look at the historical evidence that we have around us. Does that stuff line up with the Bible?

The overwhelming majority of evidence says, "Yes, without question."

In fact, there is virtually no hard archeological evidence that traces human existence and societies that would refute what the Bible says. There is a lot in the Bible that we have no archeological evidence for; I am more than willing to admit that. But I am saying if you are looking for evidence in archeology or history that would say the Bible is without a doubt wrong, you will not find that evidence.

External evidence powerfully proves the Bible can be trusted, but the *internal* evidence is probably even more powerful proof. The internal evidence says, let's look at what the Bible says about itself. Let's look at how the Bible is put together. Let's look at the claims that the Bible makes, and then the Bible goes on to fulfill those claims, meaning prophecies and how those prophecies were fulfilled or passages of Scripture that line up with one another.

I want to admit that there are some textual challenges in the Bible, but by percentage, we are talking about less than 1% of textual challenges. And in almost every one of those cases, we just do not have enough evidence to completely rule out the challenges that the Bible produces or that we find in the Bible.

Those 1% of cases do not contradict the Bible. They are just challenging parts of the Bible. So when you take the 99% of the Bible that has no textual challenges and virtually seamlessly integrates with itself, you have a really, really strong record.

No sports team would ever have a 99% winning average, and people without people saying it is a champion team. Yet when folks criticize the Bible, it will be because of a very small, minor percentage. And I would say personally that I believe even in those very small, minor areas, we just (human beings) do not have enough information. Or maybe we have not properly understood the text well enough to be able to eliminate even that really small, less than 1%.

I am perfectly comfortable saying the Bible is 100% accurate, and where I do not see or where I am confused, that is my fault, not the Bible's fault. So when you take all of the archeology, history, and the claims that the Bible makes about itself, there is no question the Bible can be trusted. In all of human history, there has never been a book that is as validated or as trustworthy as the Bible.

QUESTION #10: Where did Baptist, Methodist, and Nazarene churches come from? Do they teach something different?

The second part of the question is a lot easier to answer than the first. Yes, they have slightly different points of doctrine. 99% of what these denominations believe is in alignment with each other. The other 1% is where different denominations come from.

The first question would require hundreds of years of church history to explain, which I do not have the space for here, and you probably do not want to hear it. I just want to say that these denominations have accomplished some amazing things. But when you compare them to what a united Christian faith *could have* accomplished, I can't help but be sad by all the denominationalism in our world.

QUESTION #11: I know it seems odd, but I grew up attending a Catholic church and going to Catholic school where we were taught that you recite certain prayers, and everything is very much a ritual. I'm trying to break away from that and cultivate my own personal relationship with King Jesus. Is there a certain way that we should pray, or is just talking to Jesus and praising him or telling him my thoughts okay?

This is a beautiful question. I want to start off by saying there is absolutely nothing wrong with reciting prayers, as long as those prayers come right from the heart. Jesus taught his disciples a prayer that they recited and learned from memory. Then his disciples passed that prayer down from generation to generation. It is called the Lord's Prayer. We still recite the prayer that Jesus taught his original disciples to pray 2000 years ago.

The key is… from a sincere heart. Jesus has several stories about prayer, and he does criticize ritualistic prayer if it does not come from the heart. In fact, Jesus gives this beautiful example in one of the gospel accounts where he says two guys went up on a hill and basically went up to the Temple to pray.

One of them was a very well-educated, highly respected religious leader. And the other one was a notorious sinner. The highly-respected religious leader said this beautiful, very routine prayer. And in his prayer he talked about how good he was and how bad other people were. Then Jesus says something fascinating.

He says that the other person who is in the Temple praying is so sick at his sin, so ashamed of what he has done, that he can't even lift his eyes up to God. He humbly just cries out from a sincere heart, "God, be merciful on me. I'm a sinner."

And then Jesus makes the statement, "I tell you the truth. The sinner went home justified, not the religious leader." What I think the essence of what Jesus is getting at here is that prayer must come from a sincere heart. And if you are just saying the words, even if it is a ritual, even if it is words that are spontaneous, and they do not come from a sincere heart, God knows it.

He knows whether or not that prayer is coming from a sincere heart. God hears and he honors the sincere prayer, even the sincere prayer of a sinner, but not the very ornate prayers of a highly religious person that do not come from a sincere heart.

The idea that Jesus has given is, God does not pay any attention to those kinds of prayers. Jesus says, "When you pray, instead of going out in public and making a big show about it and getting a lot of people to tell you how awesome that prayer was, go into your closet and pray to your Father in secret, who hears your heart. He knows what is going on in your heart, and he honors that prayer done in secret."

I don't think Jesus is literally talking about a physical place of praying in the street or praying in the closet. I think what he is talking about is the motivation behind your words. Are you trying to impress people? If you are trying to impress people, that is all your prayer is going to accomplish.

Are you really pouring your heart out to a God who hears you and who wants to communicate with his children? If that is the case, what Jesus is saying is, you can do that any- where. You can do that from the belly of a great fish like Jonah did, and God can hear that prayer. So, when you pray, please pray from a sincere heart.

QUESTION #12: Can a person, faithfully serve God, call himself or herself a Christian and then vote for a Democrat who says that abortion is not immoral?

It almost sounds to me like this person is trying to argue that people should vote for a specific political party if they are Christians, that people should vote for a specific candidate for the Presidency of the United States. It does not feel like a sincere question, but more like an argument for a specific political party.

Maybe the better way to answer this question is to say, if you are asking how a Christian should vote, then I would say you must vote your conscience and not by political party. You must vote your conscience before God, knowing that God will hold all people accountable for who they put into office and who they do not put into office.

Abortion is definitely an issue that should impact Christians, and we should be highly concerned about it. It should influence the way that we vote, but abortion is not the only issue that should influence the way that we vote. There are many other social issues, moral issues (I would call them spiritual issues) that should influence the way that a Christian votes. And I will not allow Christianity to be hijacked by a specific political party in the United States.

QUESTION #13: How can Jesus be the only way to God?

This now gets to the essence of Christianity, right? This gets to the essence of the gospel. Go back to the question, how can a loving God send people to Hell? I said in the answer to that question, it is ultimately by resisting a loving God that people send themselves to Hell. I am telling you this because the answer to this question is the fundamental basic basis of Christianity.

In the Christian faith, we do not work our way into Heaven. God and God alone can change the heart of a wicked sinner like myself. And if I were to try to do good works, there is no amount of good works that I can do to earn my way into Heaven, because God requires moral perfection. Jesus is the only morally perfect man.

If you were to try to stand before God and give an account of your deeds without the blood of Jesus and the righteousness of Jesus being credited to your account, you would stand before God having committed sin. One sin, one million sins… It doesn't matter. Sin deserves punishment.

The eternal punishment of sin is death, separation from God forever. So, only by a perfect, sinless man, can others get into Heaven. Only by God taking the initiative, coming to us to clean us up, rescue us and make us righteous before God, can we possibly (sinful men and women) stand in the presence of a perfectly holy, absolutely just God.

Therefore, the only way that a person can be morally perfect and have all of his or her bad deeds wiped out is through the blood of Jesus. Jesus gives us credit for all of his good deeds. They are credited to us at salvation. That all comes through the blood of Jesus and through his perfect righteousness.

QUESTION #14: I could never take the blind leap of faith that believing in Jesus requires.

Notice, this really isn't a question. It is a statement, right? And really, what the statement is implying is, you have to believe in something against your better judgment in order to get into Heaven… Wrong!

I like to think about Christianity like a bridge. The bridge Christianity represents is the gap between sinful man and a Holy God. And Jesus, of course, *is* the bridge. His perfect, sinless life and his sacrificial death are the two directions to travel across this bridge.

But when it comes to exercising faith, there is a step that you must be willing to take that nobody can take for you. However, it is not a blind leap! There is a lot that you can and should understand before you take the step of faith in Jesus. But I would also admit that there is no amount of proof that can settle this conclusively. There is no amount of evidence that can ultimately remove that step of faith and turn it into a set of facts. That last step for some people is a huge step; for others it is a very small step. But it is a step into the unknown that trusting what you have heard about King Jesus is really true.

I am going to give you a quick illustration for this taking a step of faith. I used to tell soldiers this in the military all the time. I used to tell them it is a lot like jumping out of an airplane. Now, you can put a parachute on your back. You can get up in an airplane. You can open the doors up, and you can fly around in that airplane with the doors open for hours, telling people, "I trust this parachute. I believe that this parachute was packed by people who know what they are doing. I believe that this parachute will open and will save my life."

You can do all of those things, and I would say that you *should* be able to trust the people who packed those parachutes for you, just like you *should* be able to trust the evidence for the Bible and trust all of the testimony of people who have placed their genuine faith in Jesus.

What I told soldiers in the Army is, you really have not exercised faith until you step out of the airplane and start to fall and that parachute has a chance to open and catch you. Until that moment has happened, you really haven't taken the leap of faith. You really have not exercised faith.

I am telling you this because maybe you have heard all of the right answers. Maybe in your head you know all of the answers to all of the questions, and you believe the answers to all of the questions. But until you have taken the final step, until you have left the airplane and started to fall and allowed the parachute to open up, you really have not exercised faith.

And what God expects of his people is that we would not just know it in our heads, but we would take the final step of faith. And in our hearts, we would trust with our hearts and bet our life and our eternity on what we have in our heads, by trusting in Jesus Christ, by placing faith (or you could call it stepping over the line of faith) that believing in Jesus Christ requires.

That is something that everyone can do. And by the way, you trust things that you cannot see all of the time. You trust them in your home. You trust them in your workplace. You trust them at school. You even trust the cars that are on the road coming toward you, that the drivers won't cross over the line and crash into you head first.

We trust things all the time. And a lot of the things that we trust are not nearly as worthy of our trust as the God of the Bible and as the blood of Jesus Christ is worthy of our total trust.

QUESTION #15: How can belief in God be reconciled with science, especially with evolution?

I think this question presumes that you cannot believe in God and the theory of evolution at the same time. If that is the premise for this question, I want to just go ahead and say, that is not a foregone conclusion. Evolution is a theory. If you hold to the theory of evolution, then evolution gives you some indications of the origin of the universe. What evolution does *not* do is get all the way back to before the universe began. In other words, it offers a single point of dense matter that became the big bang, which eventually became everything in the universe.

But evolutionists cannot point back to what happened *before* time began. What happened before the first thing happened? All of that to say, evolution is still a scientific theory, and I do not think it is fair to treat scientifically the theory of evolution like it naturally excludes faith in the God of the Bible. These are two completely different types of science… Biology and Theology.

If you treat science like it is trying to answer the question WHY instead of answering the questions WHAT or HOW, you are in essence turning science into a religion. Science might answer the questions, how did the universe start, and what is it made of? Those are really important questions. But scientific observation cannot answer the *most* important question, *why* does the universe exist?

The WHY question is answered at the soul level by a faith system. When people try to put science in the category of

answering the WHY questions they have in essence, turned science into a religion. And now science has to be able to compete
by the same rules that every other religion has to compete with.

At the same time, religion is not designed to answer *all*
of the scientific questions about the origin of the universe, about
mankind, about the way that the world functions. That is not the
goal of the Bible. The Bible has a lot to say about those things,
but that is not why the Bible was written.

So, to answer this question, I am saying there does not
have to be a hard divide between science and faith. I am not using the word religion now. I have intentionally changed the language to say *faith*. All scientists start off with premises based on
faith, and then they set out to prove or disprove those premises.
In essence, Christianity is asking you to do the same thing. It
starts off with the premise that Jesus really is the son of God. He
really did live 2,000 years ago. He really did die on the cross.
And he really did come back from the grave three days later.

Like any good scientist, the next stage is up to you. And
that is to search out the evidence and see if it really supports that
kind of logic.

QUESTION #16: What about all of the contradictions in the Bible?

You have to point to exact places where somebody has told you the Bible contradicts itself in order for me to answer this question. I have spent 30 years daily (this is not an exaggeration), every day for more than 30 years, studying the Bible, looking at the truth of the Bible, and I have not found a single contradiction.

Now, I want to admit there are some places in the Bible where I struggle to understand what the Bible is saying. I have difficulties interpreting the Bible. I even struggle with the ideas or the theological implications of what some passages of the Bible say. But, in every one of those cases, I automatically default to: There is something that I do not understand; there is not something wrong with the Bible. There is something wrong with me, and I do not understand this passage. That is why this passage is confusing.

But I have honestly not found a place anywhere in the Bible that explicitly contradicts itself. And when you talk about a book written over more than a thousand years in multiple countries by scores of authors, you cannot find any other piece of human literature that you can put to that level of scrutiny and have that kind of harmony, that kind of accuracy. It is in a league all on its own.

QUESTION #17: Did the miracles that are recorded in the Bible really happen, or are they like magic tricks? Were they just simple-minded, gullible people who had the wool pulled over their eyes?

It is a good question, right? The basis for this question may be, "I've never seen a miracle. I'm not sure that I totally believe in miracles. The Bible is chock full of them. How can I believe in a miracle when I've never seen one?"

Let's just remember what the word *miracle* refers to. It is an act of God outside of nature that cannot be rationalized, cannot be explained away. Science cannot give you a definition for what just happened. And by that description, there are many, many miracles recorded in the Bible.

In fact, you could say for 40 years, every day God was doing a miracle that the Bible backs up by providing manna in the morning, a pillar of fire at night and a pillar of cloud during the day. God was visibly showing up and leading his people to the Promised Land every day for 40 years. That is just one simple example of many, many miracles in the Bible.

So now the question becomes, can you prove that these miracles happened? Well, not by using any kind of scientific measure that we have, because by definition, a miracle has to exist outside of the natural order, outside of our scientific tools and our formulas to measure it.

But let's just flip the coin over. Can you absolutely conclusively *disprove* it? If you cannot absolutely, conclusively prove a miracle, then it would be equally as difficult to absolutely conclusively disprove a miracle, unless you were there the moment that miracle happened. I believe our God still conducts miracles today, and I believe people have seen miracles with their own eyes.

I personally can attest to at least two miracles in my life. One of them is the miracle of new birth in me, when God took a dead soul and made it alive in Jesus Christ. I did not do anything for God to do that, to prompt God to do that. That was just a sovereign miracle by the all-powerful God.

So Jeff's answer is really easy to this question. Are the Bible miracles magic tricks or illusions that gullible people believe? No, they actually happened. You and I did not get a chance to see the Bible miracles with our own eyes, but that doesn't mean that they didn't happen. And we do not have any scientific instruments to measure those miracles, so we do not have any scientific measurements to disprove those miracles.

QUESTION #18: Aren't all religions a psychological crutch for weak-minded people?

This question sounds like a variation of Karl Marx's statement that religion is the "opiate of the masses". Marx believed that religion was used to dull the mind and make people easier for the government to control.

If you go and do some honest research, you will find that people of faith exhibit better mental health traits in almost every category measurable. Faith, therefore, is not a crutch for weak-minded people; it is a splint to set straight a fractured soul. You can lean on a crutch, but you can also lean on a splint. However, only the splint will straighten out what is broken.

My answer also depends on what you consider to be weak-minded. I certainly would not consider myself to be in that category. Are you talking about me? Because I would tell you that God worked an incredible miracle and made my dead heart alive, or else I would not be following him today.

At the same time, I am strong enough to admit that I lean on my faith 100% of the time. Yes, I turn to my faith to get me through the problems of life. That is what Jesus said we are supposed to do when he likened the Christian faith to "solid ground". The guy who builds his life on the sand, when life gets hard and the wind and the waves crash against it, that faith will come crumbling to the ground around him.

Essentially, Jesus is saying that the person who built his life on the solid-rock faith in him will be able to withstand the wind and waves of difficulty. Jesus is saying, "Trust in me, and I'll support you during the most challenging times." I leaned on faith in him when bullets were flying all around me and when people were dying around me. I was able to walk across the battlefield with absolutely no fear because of my faith in Jesus.

There is no psychological answer for that, except a miracle of God giving me peace in the middle of certain death. You could call that a crutch if you want, but if you have never been shot at, it would be really hard once you have been in the circumstances I have been in to consider that a crutch used by a weak-minded person.

QUESTION #19: Can Christianity be proved?

No. That is the short answer to the question. Neither can it be disproved. I tell people you do not have to check your brain at the door and that Christianity is a reasonable faith. By reasonable, I mean that you can reason and understand the history, the theology, the ethics and the archeology of the Christian faith. Many of the claims of Jesus can be researched. The more research you do, the more it will point to the truth of the Bible and the claims of Jesus.

But faith, by definition, cannot be conclusively proved or disproved. You have to choose to believe or choose not to believe. No amount of evidence will eliminate the need for the final step of faith. God created it this way.

For example, in Luke chapter 16, Jesus tells a parable of a rich man and Lazarus. He says that after the rich man died, he went to torment in Hell. Lazarus, on the other hand, died and went to Heaven. The rich man asked God to send Lazarus back from the grave and warn his living brothers about the torment waiting for them in Hell if they do not turn their lives around.

Jesus's parable in Luke 16 answers this question. Jesus said that no one can go from Heaven over to Hell. No one can go from Hell to Heaven. And people do not go from Heaven back to Earth. He said instead that they have the Bible; the Bible has all we need to know about faith.

Then, for emphasis, Jesus says, "If they will not believe the Scriptures, they will not believe even if a guy like Lazarus returns from the grave." Jesus is saying that God created Christianity in such a way that you are ultimately going to have to take the last step by faith. Do the research. Check out the faith. You will be amazed at how many of the claims of the Bible can be validated. But the last step is always going to be a step of faith, and God intentionally created it that way.

QUESTION #20: If Christianity is so great, then why are there so few Christians in the world?

That is a really powerful question that deserves a really honest answer. I will give you a one-word answer: Cost. More people do not follow Jesus because they understand the cost. Following Jesus is going to cost you less than you think and more than you can possibly imagine.

I think some people start to realize what it is going to cost them, and when they realize that, they decide, "You know what? I'm not willing to give that up. And so, as great as Christianity sounds, I'm just not willing to make that trade."

More than once while sharing my faith with my friends in the military, I explained the gospel in a way that they heard it and understood it. When I offered them a chance to respond to Christ in faith, several of them said, "I'm not going to do that."

I asked them, "Don't you understand what's at stake here? Don't you understand what will happen if you don't surrender your life to Christ?" And they said, "Oh, I heard what you said, and I completely understand it." Their very honest answer to me was, "I'm not willing to give up my sin. I like my sin too much. And if I understood you correctly, I would have to be willing to give up my sin in order to become a Christian."

Now, what I wanted them to understand is, you don't do that. Jesus puts something in your heart that makes you no longer *want* to sin. But what they concluded was, "It's going to cost me my sin, and I enjoy my sin right now. I'm not willing to make that trade, so I'm just going to go on with my life, understanding the consequences that it may cost me eternity in Hell."

This is the reason why a lot of people are not Christians right now. They may never say it out loud, but they really *do* understand what it would cost them.

QUESTION #21: How can you know there is a God?

I am just going to go ahead and answer this question with a very short answer and then explain. You cannot *know* that there is a God through objective, scientific measurements.

"Knowing" God is an act of faith- if you take the biblical word 'know' to mean intimate knowledge. I think all of the evidence points strongly to the existence of God. When you look at the evidence from history, archeology, or even biology points to the existence of God. However, God ordered faith in such a way that we must come to him in faith. If you could prove his existence with 100% evidence, then it would not be faith.

My friend Ken Keathley points out the famous philosopher Blaise Pascal's answer to this question: God reveals himself sufficiently so that anyone who wishes to believe, can; and that he has sufficiently hidden himself so that no one is compelled to believe. Thus, belief becomes a moral choice for which we are all held accountable.

QUESTION #22: How can God be good when there is so much evil in the world?

This is a classic theological difficulty. I am not going to try to avoid the question, because I believe it is a really good question that deserves an answer. I also want to say up front that for hundreds, if not thousands, of years, really smart people have wrestled with this question.

The Bible is overwhelmingly clear. God is sovereign. He is in control of everything. The Bible is equally clear that God is also good. In fact, he is all good, which means every source of good comes from him. But the Bible does not hold back the fact that there is also a lot of suffering in the world.

And because this question has been asked for centuries, this also means that there is not one overarching, succinct answer that will settle this question. The question is a tough one to answer, but it is not impossible. The answer lies in the fact that God has created the world in such a way that people chose sin and rebellion rather than following Jesus.

If there is genuinely an opportunity for people to deny God and rebel against him, if he really created a world in such a way that his own creatures could turn their backs on him, and his own creatures can destroy the paradise that God created by their own sin, then all of the suffering and all of the evil in the world, is our fault. We cannot blame it on God.

God created perfect harmony in the Garden of Eden. - perfect harmony with him, harmony between people, and har-

mony with nature. All three of those relationships were broken
when Adam and Eve committed the first sin. Their relationship
with God was broken, their relationship with each other was
broken, and even the earth itself was cursed, according to Genesis 3. So even natural disasters are the result of sin.

But I also must say, there will be a time when God will
restore all that was destroyed by sin in the Garden of Eden. The
problem of evil will be solved when God ushers in the new age,
restores the new Jerusalem, and restores everything to the way it
was supposed to be. The Bible is very clear that this will be the
moment when there will be no more suffering. There will be no
more sickness. There will be no more sin. I realize that is probably less satisfying of an answer than you wanted, but that is the
truth, and it is a question that people have wrestled with for centuries.

QUESTION #23: Does it really matter what you believe as long as you are sincere in what you believe?

Beautiful question. And the one word answer to the question is: yes.

It absolutely matters. Let me use an analogy to explain my answer. If you and I were standing at the top of a skyscraper and you said, "I really sincerely believe that I could jump off of this building without a parachute and I would be able to land safely on the ground," it does not matter how sincere that belief is. When you jump off of that building, if you do not have a parachute, you are going to die.

Many people have sincerely and totally believed something that was a lie. And when you realize that it is a lie, it hurts. It doesn't matter how sincere your belief, it is still a lie.

This is also true of faith. The Christian faith teaches that you cannot work hard enough or be religious enough to get to Heaven by your own effort. Virtually all other faith systems give some form of working hard to achieve Nirvana/Paradise/Valhalla/Enlightenment or whatever it is. There is nothing compatible with those different faith systems. They are absolutely at odds with one another. This is the proof that it matters what you believe.

No matter how sincere your faith, you cannot jump off a skyscraper and land safely. You would be sincerely wrong. Two beliefs that are completely contradictory to one another themselves answer the question, does it matter what you believe as long as you are sincere? Every other world religion contradicts the essence of Christianity. You cannot sincerely believe both of them and still be right.

QUESTION #24: What is Christian conversion? Can it be explained psychologically?

Can Christian conversation be explained using psychological terms? No. That is the one-word answer to the question. As to the first question, what is it? The best language I could use to explain conversion is a *supernatural change of the heart and will*.

At conversion, the Holy Spirt of God works with our spirit granting us repentance from sin, and faith in Jesus Christ as savior. That is what a Christian conversion looks like from the viewpoint of the "converted".

Because Christian conversion is part of the supernatural work of God in the heart of a Christian, there is no way to classify it as a psychological phenomenon. There are certainly emotional, spiritual and psychological aspects to conversion. However, Christian conversion is ultimately a work of God in the human heart and will.

QUESTION #25: Can you prove that Christianity is the truth?

Well, at the risk of sounding contradictory… sort of. If you read my response to the question about proving the existence of God, you will see that I argued that there is 99% proof. There is enough evidence that I believe 99% proof, but the last 1% remaining is an act of faith.

But this is a different question. When asked, "Can we prove Christianity?" my answer to this is going to be, perhaps. It depends on your definition of the word "proof". Would one person's life being radically changed to the point that he or she is willing to sell everything, move halfway around the world and spend the rest of his or her life telling people how Jesus saved them? Is that proof enough for you? That radical behavior seems like conclusive proof to me, because there is no satisfactory explanation for this kind of behavior.

What if it was a billion or two billion people who were so convinced about something that their lives were radically changed by it? What if it was *many* billions of people over thousands of years? Would that prove to you that Christianity is true? But maybe here is the greatest proof.

If a man who was dead, who claimed to have the power over life or death, took up the power over death and came back out of the grave on his own, would that prove to you that Christianity is true? It was proof enough for Jesus's own brothers and his sister. Mark 3 suggests that Jesus's family previously believed that there was something psychologically off with him.

And they were going to take him home and take care of him because they thought that he was off his rocker by the statements he was making publicly.

And then his brothers, two of them at least, if not all of them, were radically changed. They were so radically changed, in fact, that they were willing to give their lives up, because now they believed that their brother really was the son of God.

James and Jude, who wrote Bible books, are Jesus's half-brothers. Before his death and resurrection, they thought he was crazy. After his death and resurrection, they are completely convinced that he is the son of God and are willing to sacrifice their lives to tell people about him. I think that is the proof that verifies Christianity. James and Jude are proof that validates everything that Jesus said about himself.

QUESTION #26: What about the Trinity? Do Christians worship three gods?

No. We only worship one God, who has eternally manifested himself in three persons. But you are also asking in the first question, what is the Trinity?

Now, I am just going to tell you, this is a really, really hard concept to describe, even for a PhD theologian. It is a challenge because there is really nothing in the universe that is comparable to our God. Therefore, nothing perfectly demonstrates the concept of the Trinity, which means any kind of analogy I use to explain the Trinity is going to be insufficient.

However, just because I do not have the words to completely explain the Trinity doesn't make it false. It really should not come as a surprise that there are some things about God that our finite minds are unable to totally grasp or that human language is incapable of exhaustively describing.

The Bible is abundantly clear: "Hear O Israel, the Lord, our God, the Lord is one." One God, the Father, Son, and Holy Spirit, who has manifested himself perfectly in three persons. For all of eternity, before creation began, the Father, Son, and Holy Spirit existed. After time ceases to exist, the Father, Son, and Holy Spirit will always be perfectly, completely one God manifested in three persons.

QUESTION #27: If God already knows the outcome of our existence, does that mean that we really never had a choice?

Good question. Here is another way to ask it: "Does God know our outcome, but allows us to choose anyway? And if he knows what our choice is going to be, do we really have a choice, in reality?" The answer in short is… Yes!

I am going to answer your question, but first I want to ask you to consider the chronology of what you are saying. I want you to think about this through the lens of time. Everything that we know, all of our life, has always existed within the framework of time. From the first day of creation, when God created the Heavens and the Earth and said, "Let there be light," that is when the human clock started ticking. And all humans have ever known from the very beginning of our existence is influenced by time. But God is not limited by time like we are.

Peter describes God's view as a day being like 1,000 years and 1,000 years as like a day in 2 Peter 3, meaning that time as we know it is not the way God recognizes time. So when you ask about God's knowledge of events, technically you are asking about God's foreknowledge. This is where using a modern human understanding of time to think about and understand a God who is not constrained by time becomes problematic.

Now admittedly, God acts within time. After all, at the perfect time, God sent forth his son. God starts something, continues something, and sees it to conclusion. And the Bible references God moving inside of the nature he created, doing miracles that are timely miracles.

Please forgive this academic discussion about time, but it is really important to what you just asked. God knows the beginning, middle and the end all at the same time. You and I can only understand where we are in this moment in time and where we have been in the past, but we cannot recognize the future. For God, there is no future. For God, there is no past. For God, there is no present. It is always the future, always the past, and always the present.

God created a world in such a way that time exists, and he will one day, by the way, at the end of the age, do away with time. That is why there are no clocks in Heaven. There is no measure for eternity.

Okay, that is a lot of explanation for your question. Yes, God already knows the outcome before we choose. But the fact that he already knows the outcome does not necessarily preclude the fact that we had a choice in the first place.

QUESTION #28: How are we as Christians supposed to love sinners without appearing to approve of their sin?

This is admittedly hard, because there is overt approval and then there is tacit approval. Overt approval of sin is like saying, "Oh, it's no big deal. God doesn't care." Giving overt approval of sin dishonors a Holy God. But most of us do not struggle with overt approval of sin. Most Christians (myself included) struggle with tacit approval of sin.

Many Christian want to know if it is okay to be around when sin is going on. What if I am around sin, and I don't say something about it, or I don't stop it? That is a much harder question to answer. In this case, every situation is a little bit different. In fact, even very sincere Christians have different opinions based on the situation.

I believe this is the issue that some Pharisees were wrestling with while watching the crowd Jesus hung with. They said, "How can you be a religious leader if you are around these sinners? That woman who is touching you right now, Jesus, if you really were the son of God, you would know what kind of woman this is who is touching you. So either you don't know, which means you're not the son of God, or you don't care, which means you're not a very good Messiah."

Jesus's answer might answer your question. He says, "Hey, the healthy people don't need a doctor; sick people do. I've come to earth to be around sick people, and you healthy people, you go back to your books and go back to your religious accusations and your judgment of others. I'm here to be around sinners."

I think the best answer to your question is to follow Jesus's example. He never tolerates sin. He looks at the woman caught in adultery and says, "Go and sin no more." But he also does not push her away. He does not overtly excuse sin, but he also does not avoid sinners.

I think somewhere in there is the right combination, but I would admit I struggle in some circumstances or situations knowing what the right thing to do is. I am trying to honor Jesus and also let the sinner know that I love him or her, while not giving the impression that I am okay with the sinful act he or she is doing.

QUESTION #29: Is there legitimate evidence against the virgin birth?

I am going to say no, based on the way that the question is worded. When you say *legitimate evidence* and *virgin birth* at the same time, please consider what you just did with the English language. If you ask, "Is it possible that the virgin birth didn't happen?" then my answer is… of course.

When you said, "Is there evidence against the virgin birth?" there are accusations and some arguments suggesting why it did not happen. When you asked for evidence against the virgin birth, now the answer becomes really precise. You are asking for evidence that a miracle *did not* happen. No amount of scientific evidence can prove or disprove a miracle. By definition, a miracle is beyond conclusive evidence.

The term "virgin birth" is miraculous language. I am trying not to insult your intelligence. Anyone with a basic understanding of the English language and human reproduction knows that virgin birth is impossible. When the Bible says that a virgin gave birth, it is saying that a miracle took place.

I should say that if the question were different, then my answer would be different. There is a story about Jesus's birth that circulated during his lifetime. Many scholars believe that this is the context for John 8:41. Many church historians believe this claim goes back to the first century. Perhaps it was started by the religious leaders as an attempt to discredit the virgin birth.

Some claimed that Mary had relations with a Roman soldier and that Jesus is the child of a Roman soldier. That is why Joseph was going to give her a certificate of divorce. That argument is still circulating around today. The Bible does not give any credibility to not just that argument, but any other way of describing Jesus's birth but an immaculate conception.

The argument FOR the virgin birth has much more credibility. It has a lot of strength because the Jews had a very clear idea from the Prophet Isaiah of how the Messiah was going to show up. I do not think they expected it to be by this teenage girl by the name of Mary and a baby in a manger, but they knew where he was going to be born, and they knew he would be born to a virgin hundreds of years before his birth.

When you put all of those factors together, it is really hard to read something different into the Bible. It is really hard to argue anything other than a virgin birth because of the overwhelming amount of evidence. The people who do argue against it basically just say, "Yeah, the virgin birth is in the Bible, but that part isn't true."

QUESTION #30: Can you be certain that you're on your way to Heaven?

In light of eternity, this is the only question that really matters, right? Yes, you can be certain that you are on your way to Heaven!

The proof is found in 1 John 2:3. Jesus gives the impression multiple times when he is speaking to audiences that you can know that you are a child of God, that you can know that you are on your way to Heaven. Paul gives the impression in his letters in multiple places that you can know that you are on your way to Heaven, but John just says it explicitly in 1 John 2:3.

John is writing his letter to Christians when he says, "This is how we _know_ that we know him [Jesus], if we keep his commands [emphasis added]." By the way, Jesus says the same thing in John 8:31.

What John is saying is, God works a supernatural miracle in your heart when you become a Christian. This changed heart wants to keep his commands. God sends his Holy Spirit to work within his people so that they can keep his commands. He first changes our desires and makes us want to keep the commandments. Second, he gives us the supernatural help by his Holy Spirit to keep his commands.

Can you be sure? Yes. The Bible says you can be sure, and it even tells you _how_ you can be sure in 1 John 2:3. The same Bible author makes it abundantly clear that you can "know" with certainty of your salvation in 1 John 5:13.

QUESTION #31: Did Jesus ever claim to be God?

Yes, clearly in the gospel of John, chapter 10. He was so clear that the religious leaders said, "Okay, we don't need to hear any more. Kill this man on the spot because of what he just said."

In John 10:22, this festival of dedication took place in Jerusalem. Jesus was walking into the Temple through Solomon's Colonnade. In Solomon's Colonnade, the Jews surrounded him and asked, "How long are you going to keep us in suspense? Are you the Messiah?" That word means, "Are you the anointed of God? Are you the son of God or not? Are you God made into flesh or not? Tell us plainly." Jesus answers using crystal clear language in his day. Today, 2,000 years later living in a different culture from Jesus, it doesn't feel as clear, but here is what he says:

In verse 25 Jesus is saying, "I did tell you, and you do not believe. The works I do in my Father's name testify about me. If you want proof, just look at what I am doing. I'm healing the sick. I'm giving sight to the blind. I'm helping people who are deaf to hear. I'm raising people from the dead. Do you know anybody else who can do that?"

Then he says this: "I told you, but you didn't believe because you are not my sheep. My sheep hear my voice. I know them, and they follow me. I give them [listen to what he says] eternal life, and they will never perish." That is something God in Heaven alone can do, and they know it.

Here is what he says next: "And no one will snatch them out of my hands." Verse 29: "My Father who has given them to me is greater than all. No one is able to snatch them out of my Father's hands." You might say, "I still don't hear it, Jeff. I'm looking for the explicit answer to the question." Well, John 10:30 says, "*I and the Father are one.*"

In the original language, Jesus just used the "I Am" name for God. This is the proper name for God. Jesus uses that name to refer to himself. Jesus says, "I and my Father are one." In other words, he is saying "I Am" the son of God. But please don't stop reading there. Look at verse 31. The Jews heard exactly what he said, and there was absolutely no mistake in their minds, because in verse 31 they picked up rocks to put him to death.

They believed he just committed blasphemy. When they asked, "Are you the son of God?", he answered, "I Am," using God's proper name. They responded by trying to punish him for blasphemy. Yeah, Jesus makes no bones about it in John 10:30, "Yep. I am the son of God."

QUESTION #32: What is the difference between denominations, especially between Catholic and Protestant denominations?

Wow! Where do I start? You just asked a question that would require a summary of 2,000 years of church history. The answer to this question could fill up entire buildings (not entire books, but entire buildings of books).

At its essence, Catholicism teaches that Jesus is the son of God, and when Jesus was leaving earth, he handed the keys to the kingdom to Peter. It teaches that Peter is the first Pope, and the keys to Heaven have passed to every other Pope after Peter. Also, the Pope has the authority to really decide who gets into Heaven and who does not.

Please forgive me, because these are gross (and by gross I mean, very big) generalizations, and any time you make really big generalizations, it offends people because there are a lot of nuances in there that I just do not have time to discuss. One of the other really big differences is, Catholics would believe in the same Bible that we believe in, though their Bible has several additional books.

Protestants would use the big theological term *pseudepigrapha* to refer to the other books in the Roman Catholic version of the Bible. One other big difference is the importance of church councils. Traditionally, Roman Catholic leadership would say, "Yes, we believe the Bible, but we also believe that our church councils are without error, and when the Pope speaks *ex cathedra,* he is also without error."

If there is ever an argument between the Bible and a church council, then typically speaking, Catholic leadership will err on the side of church teachings or church councils, meaning placing church council authority over the Bible. Because of that, you have many practices in Catholicism that are very different from Protestantism. Many of those practices come from church councils, not necessarily from the Scriptures. That is why there are so many differences.

I am trying to be both honest and succinct with my answer. There is so much more that needs to be said about this.

QUESTION #33: How do I become a Christian?

The answer to that is, by a radical, total surrender to Jesus Christ as Lord of your life.

By this I mean coming to him and trusting in him and nothing else to make you right with God. When I say nothing, I mean not even trusting in your own good works to earn your way into Heaven. Total surrender means not trusting in being religious, praying hard, reading the Bible, or even giving a lot of money is going to get you into Heaven. It is trusting only in the sacrificial death and the physical bodily resurrection of Jesus Christ. Those are the basics, but there is actually a little bit more to it than that.

It is essentially saying, "God, if you don't do a miracle in my heart, I have no hope of Heaven. I am so desperate that I am asking you to do for me what I cannot do for myself. God, please make my dead soul alive. God, would you (2 Corinthians 5:17) make me into a new creature so that the old me has passed away, and I am made new?" Through this simple surrender, God moves in his sovereign grace and does a miracle of new birth in your life.

How do you become a Christian? -by radically, totally turning to God and saying, "I have nothing to offer you. I am totally desperate. God, would you hear my prayer? Would you send your Holy Spirit to change my soul and to make me born again? And Jesus, from this moment forward, you are Lord of my life. You call the shots in my life. I don't."

Maybe you have never totally surrendered. Perhaps you are thinking, *I understand what the Bible says. I even believe a lot of what the Bible says. But if that's what it takes to become a Christian, I know I've never done that.*

Maybe you need to totally surrender to King Jesus right now. What I would like to do is just lead you in the prayer. There is no magic in these words, but if they come from a sincere heart, God hears your prayer. I believe he will sovereignly and supernaturally makes your dead soul alive if you are sincere in this prayer. If you are serious about this, would you pray this prayer?

> *God in Heaven, I am a sinner, and I can't work hard enough to earn my way into Heaven. I believe you love me, and you didn't want to leave me in my sin. So, you sent your son, Jesus, to rescue me.*

> *Jesus, who lived a perfect life, was willing to pay the price for my rescue by dying on a cross. I believe that they took that dead body off of the cross and laid him in a tomb. I also believe that three days later, he came out of the tomb alive.*

> *God, right here, right now, I am turning from my sins and turning to you. I'm asking you to clean me up. I'm asking you to do a miracle in my soul. I'm also asking you to start to give me abundant life right now, here on earth. I surrender to Jesus. I will follow him wherever my life goes next. He is my King. I pray this in Jesus name. Amen.*

If you made that commitment and you are really serious about it, I believe with every fiber of my being that God heard that prayer from Heaven and that God will supernaturally change you. We would love to follow up with you. We would love to help you understand what to do next by introducing you to our Basic Training digital course.

Visit 2citieschurch.com to sign up for this free training.

ABOUT THE AUTHOR

At age 18, Jeff enlisted in the United States Army as an Infantryman and retired as a chaplain with over 22 years of active federal service. In 2017, he was inducted into the US Army Ranger Hall of Fame.

He served for ten years in the 75th Ranger Regiment in positions from Private to Platoon Sergeant. While serving in this unit, Jeff competed in and won the David L. Grange Best Ranger Competition in 1996. He taught ROTC at the University of Louisville and was recognized in 1998 as the US Army ROTC, Noncommissioned Officer of the Year. Jeff spent his final ten years in the US Army serving as a chaplain in Airborne and Ranger units.

Some of his awards include the Ranger Tab, Combat Infantryman's Badge, Pathfinder Badge, Master Parachutists Wings, Military Freefall Master Parachutist Wings, several foreign jump wings and the Combat Action Badge. His combat experience includes participation in the invasion of Panama, Operation Desert Storm, Black Hawk Down in Somalia, and more than a dozen combat tours in Afghanistan and Iraq. Jeff has been awarded medals for valor in combat.

Jeff holds a Ph.D. from Southeastern Baptist Theological Seminary in Wake Forest, NC. He also has several other earned and honorary degrees.

He is the lead pastor of 2 Cities Church in Columbus, Georgia, an in-demand event speaker, and he is an award-winning author with five other books in print.